Føund in Tränšlatioñ

Føund in Tränšlation

A extremely guide to
speak correctly English

*

Tomas Santos

Michael O'Mara Books Limited

First published in Great Britain in 2010 by
Michael O'Mara Books Limited
9 Lion Yard
Tremadoc Road
London SW4 7NQ

The text of this book is partly based on the author's *Speak Well
English: An guide for aliens to successful intercourse in the correctly English
mode*, published by Michael O'Mara Books Limited in 2004.

A CIP catalogue record for this book is available from the British Library.

Papers used by Michael O'Mara Books Limited are natural, recyclable products
made from wood grown in sustainable forests. The manufacturing processes
conform to the environmental regulations of the country of origin.

ISBN: 978-1-84317-442-4

1 3 5 7 9 10 8 6 4 2

www.mombooks.com

Typeset and designed by www.glensaville.com

Printed in the UK by CPI Mackays, Chatham, ME5 8TD

I should like much devoted this book my mother and to my home land that I lived when I was infantile. It was the country of milk and syrup. I darling it.

TOMAS SANTOS

INSIDES CONTENT

Contents

PUBLISHER'S PREFACE

When it comes to choosing the right person to compile an English phrasebook for foreigners, Tomas Santos does not spring to mind as the most obvious candidate. It would be an understatement to describe his grasp of the English language as shaky and this fundamental shortcoming has not been mitigated by his reliance, in the compilation of this book, on an exotic variety of ancient phrasebooks and dictionaries through which our lovely language has been dragged backwards.

Tomas's method, it seems, has been to take idiomatic expressions which he has seen or heard in his mother tongue and translate them into English against their will, by sheer physical force. The result is a mishmash of monstrosity and beauty, in which a vocabulary of occasionally exquisite loveliness mingles with the gallimaufry of linguistic half-breeds that are the accidental love-children of the Santos translation process.

As a guide to making yourself understood *Found in Translation* is worse than useless but as an aid to cheerfulness, it is a diamond of the first water. For, while cursed with a profound ignorance of his subject, Tomas Santos is blessed with a gift for the inspired guess. Surely few readers will be unable to recognize such familiar English phrases as, 'I think I will be vomit', 'Can you recommend the best tart in your establishment', or, 'Do you serve faggots?'.

An inspirational selection of Tomas's vocabulary, proverbs

and idioms are sprinkled about the book and it is an enriching experience to unearth from the slag such nuggets as: 'If it is not busted, not repair them', 'Do not examine at a gratuitous horse in hers throat', or the profound, 'Make with others because would make you make them with you'. What better motto could any of us ask for?

The editors have left alone the unusual spellings, neologisms and mind-crunching gobbledegook with which this book is strewn, motivated partly by a concern for their own well-being. They are robust professionals but there's only so much anyone can take and they felt, after reading the manuscript a few times and taking the advice of experts in the field of mental health, that prolonged exposure would not be good for them.

You have been warned.

A NOTE ON THE LETTERS

Tomas Santos was just a boy when he first came to England in the 1980s. He lodged with his Aunt Úrsula in leafy Muswell Hill, where he received his very first English lessons, and it was here that he wrote the first of his letters – to Sherlock Holmes. Although this youthful attempt bears the tell-tale fingerprints of the apprentice correspondent, it is unmistakably Santos, containing several of the unique characteristics that were to become hallmarks of his writing in later years.

Tomas seems to have believed Sherlock Holmes to be a real

person, and this misapprehension was not cleared up when he received a friendly reply from 221b Baker Street. Indeed it was probably this small kindness, by an employee of the building society then occupying premises at that address, which lit the slow fuse that was to set off an explosion of correspondence in later years, when Tomas returned to England as a full-time English student. During this latter period he wrote boxloads of letters in between lectures, only a brief selection of which appear in this book. The Sherlock Holmes letter is here, of course, along with the reply, as are some of the last Tomas wrote before returning to his homeland to set up his own language school.

Goethe remarked that letters are among the most significant memorials a person can leave behind him, and while those of Tomas Santos may not be up there with Pliny the Younger, they do make wonderful reading and tell us quite a lot about the eager young man who so earnestly composed them.

A CORRESPONDENCE TO THE PRIVATE DICK

112 Muswell Hill Road
London
N10 3JD

5nd January 1988

Mr Sherlock Homes
221b Baker Street
London

Dear Mr Sherlock Holmes
  I am in this country since only four months to study
the English in your country. I now speak almost well and
so I am reading a borrowed storey of you and called The
Hound of The Baskervilges. She is a most exiting storey of
many goods moments .
  My teacher English is a great liker of you thrilling
tails and say to me to writing you in the addres he have
gived me in Bakers Street.
  Can you to send me a singed photograph perhaps with
you and Miss Hudson and Mr Doctor Dr Waston in? This will
made me most pleased indeed.
  I send to you my wish for this new year of 1988 and I
greet you with my feelings. I am desolate this letter is
quite bad typing .

Yours friend

TOMAS SANTOS

BS. What you put in you pipe? Do you and Dr Watson like a
rough shag by the fire?

7th January 1988

Dear Tomas Santos

Mr Holmes thanks you for your letter and has asked me to reply on his behalf.

He regrets that he is unable to comply with your specific request, as you may be aware, Mr Holmes has now retired to Sussex where he spends his time reviewing the records of his cases and keeping bees.

In his own words, Mr Holmes has given himself up entirely: "to that soothing life of Nature for which I had so often yearned during the long years spent amid the gloom of London."

He is nevertheless, delighted to be the recipient of such vast amounts of mail every week and sends you his cordial regards.

            Yours sincerely

            Nikki Caparn
      Secretary to Sherlock Holmes

PRELUDE BY TOMAS SANTOS

Hello.

When I visited firstly in England all was foreign and the queer native startled me with his tongue. I nevertheless worked in my language college extremely to understand him, and after always a hard day I tossed myself onto the mattress with exhaust. My education was consequently in a twinkling accomplished, and I speaked so well English that I wished to help another learning person shall speak correctly also it. I had already some phrase books but they was incomprehending, so I made my mind to wrote at once the best one phrase book you ever want.

In my home land it was never allowed to had the seditious writing in one's houses so always I hided my papers in the hole in my uncle's back passage. But soon, as time went away, I came in England and I now here have wrote it. My notorious book calls herself *Found in Translation – a extremely guide to speak correctly English*. She book will empower the learning tourist, or the voracious novice, to flourish at once for acquire fluency English – notwithstanding inferior initial knowings. Therefore all aliens now should had pleasure from the English tongue and made successful intercourse with natives in the correctly English mode.

All pupil should wish he shall got better in the promptly fashion and *Found in Translation* are give you the unique helpment. May be it is that you are newly visiting in UK and can don't speak English. Then here book is aimed on you.

Inside is the commonplace discourses, such that *Under the barber*, *To the pub*, or *In the hostel*, with, as well to that, some useful sayings and assortment vocabularies for repetitious instruction. So if you will study her closely you shall at once forgot that native ejaculations are foreign in your mouth, and shall speak a flowing English like a congenital native.

Furthermore, among this book will you found a spattering of my letters who I wrote them to English gentlemans and ladies to gave me advice to be more British. There is the Queen (Elizabeth III), David Beckham (a soccer fan), the Archbishop Canterbury, and some others ones that I forgot. I put as well theirs responding letters and I hope you will interested thems.

I wished ultimately such that if you want to learn English badly, *Found in Translation* will teach you a lesson. Therefore, as the English drinking salute said it: *Cheerio to your good health, and up your bottoms!*

Yours friend

Tomas Santos

COMMONPLACE DISCOURSES

The most superlative method to learn of language is jump on the deep end. They realistic dialogues such that are afterwards printed allow the callow pupil to play with the English tongue and lick any problem.

IN THE RESTAURANT

The UK restaurants shall serve you old food such that roasted beef of old England, pig heads eating the apple, streak and kidney pies, and cock in wine. If you finished with a spotted dick I hope you will be fed up.

THE DISCOURSE

Good night, Hotelmaster. I have reversed a table.

Welcome in our restaurant, Sir. Your table is for five covers equipped. The waiter shall here in a minute.

No, Hotelmaster, he must attend me at once.

Very good, Sir, he comes now.

Thank. I see him.

What do you want, Mister?

This bread sticks is inferior, boy. I wish another directly.

Accept this replacements, Sir. Also here is yours menus. Shall you drink?

Get us best wine.

Very well. The wine smellier comes quickly to explain his tipples. Will you take a bottle lively water?

No, we should burp ourselves. Tell us, my dear fellow, do you have crabs?

Desolately, they is not of season.

Well, how are your calves?

Ever well.

Super.

Are you then made up?

Yes. We shall begin of some porn cocktail and we will then eat your rabbits, grouses, and peasants cremated in a custard. My sister is on the game – she would take the 'Coq With Hares and Wine in a Fireburnt Sauce'. Will you inflame him on the table that we may see the wonder?

No.

Then cook our goose.

That was a delicious table, Waiter. I am repleted.

Good news, Sir. Shall you desire more any items?

Kindly ignite my cigar only and deliver me the addings check.

My pleasure. Service ain't included. I bid you farewell.

USEFUL SAYINGS IN THE RESTAURANT

Do you serve faggots?

Why are these plates *square*?

This chicken is rubbery. Look at my wife's breasts.

My desert is too much hot. Give me cold cream.

My lady wants stuffing.

Is this lobster or crap?

My salad is wanting, waiter. Put a dress on.

Did you desire me to pass water Madam?

A CORRESPONDENCE TO THE BUTCHERS

'Snaresbrooke'
2 Nevill Gardens
Hove, BN3 7QF

3nd November 2002

Graham Sharp Esq.
The Clerk to the Worshipful Company of Butchers
Butchers' Hall
87 Bartholomew Close
London
EC1A 7EB

Dear Mr Sharp

Did you knew you have the appropriate name?

I am visiting in England to study of English and to made money for my student learning's I work in the butcher but I do not slaughter myself. There also is another one assistant. She is an beginner so I showed her to hold my chopper. She is learning only, but one day I think she will pull it off.

How may I to became associated to yours worshipful company? (may also the woman join?)

Sincerely yours friend

TOMAS SANTOS

THE WORSHIPFUL COMPANY OF BUTCHERS

Tomas Santos, Esq.,
"Snaresbrooke",
2, Nevill Gardens,:
Hove, BN3 7QF

11th November 2002

Dear Mr Santos,

The Clerk, Graham Sharp, has passed to me your letter of
3rd November.

I am not sure as to how you wish to become associated with THe
Butchers' Company but would advise as a start that you consider becoming
a Member of The WCB/IoM Guild. The Guild is a Membership Organisation
with a fee, currently £49-50 per year.

Each Member reeives a Membership Certificate bearing the Armorial
Arms of The Company and signed by The Master and Clerk. Whilst a paid up
Member the Certificate may be displayed in the shop or other appropriate
premises as is the wish of the member.

Enclosed is a brochure containg an application form and which explains
Guild Membership functions. You will see that articles of topical interest
are printed in the Newsletter/Bulletin circulated to Members' quarterly
and lectures/presentations and visits to appropriate venues are made some
4 or 5 times a year.

With respect to the young lady employee you mention. The Butchers'
Companyhas no jurisdiction over a members' employees, it being entirely
the responsibility of the employer. I wonder if you and she might be
interested in her gaining meat trade qualifications. The Meat Training
Council is the Awarding Body and should this be of interest I will
arrange for full information to be forwarded. Assuming the young lady
does gain qualification(s) there are grades of Guild Membership for
which she would qualify.

I hope that the above is helpful and should you require further
information please contact me.

Yours sincerely,

F.J. Mallion, MBE.,
Past Master

'Snaresbrooke'
2 Nevill Gardens
Hove, BN3 7QF

13nd November 2002

F. J. Mallionmbe Esq.
Past Master the Worshipful Company of Butchers
Butchers' Hall
87 Bartholomew Close
London
EC1A 7EB

Dear Past Master Mallionmbe

Thank you your intersting letter.

That girl required no 'meat training'. She already can handle my meat well.

Good luck with your sausages.

Sincerely yours friend

TOMAS SANTOS

UNDER A BARBER

The hairs dresser of Great Britain shall wish to cut you very badly, and serve you right too. He is marked by the striped post and, similar to drivers of taxi, all barber have pleasure to discuss the problems of the world. Relax while he does his toilet on you.

THE DISCOURSE

Well morning my hairs expert.

To see you!

Can you strim me?

Unhappily I must cut this gentleman in front of you. But wait in a moment and I shall attend you by and by. You may pursue some the magazine or a news paper in my banquette.

I will him. Oh bother! These journals are elderly.

Sir, I am yet prepared. Sit you and I should cover you with a membrane. Now what may I do?

Crop my hairs if you please, and toilet me.

Not at all, I can it at once.

Will you shave me also?

I will him. Did you saw the soccer in the TV?

No, I went in Croydon. What squad you endorse?

Manchester Untied.

Never mind. Have your completed my hairs even?

See in my looking glass. How like you thems?

You have mussed it. You must give me a blow job and wave it.

Very well. Should I anoint you or colour in the grey threads?
Not it. But I would smell nice. Please squirt my tonsure with a odour. In another matter, had you something to the week end?

You rogue, sir! Here are some. Now must you oblige my moneys.
How many?

Sixteen euros.
Here you were. See you latter.

No doubt.

USEFUL SAYINGS IN THE BARBER

Please stop tickle me.

I never go in another barbers to got my hairs ruined – I come here.

Tissue me.

Take caution! You cut on my ear somewhat.

A CORRESPONDENCE TO THE BARBERS

2 Nevill Gardens
Hove, BN3 7QF

3st November 2002

Brigadier Alan Eastburn
Clerk to the Worshipful Company of Barbers
Barber-Surgeons' Hall
Monkwell Square
Wood Street
London
EC2Y 5BL

Dear Brigadier Eastbum

In my home land I made to barber in my village. We gave every service: short backsides, the waving, and the blow job. Ours motto had been: 'We want to cut you very badly – and serve you right too!' I gave people always the proper 'seeing to' in my home land. Our tools always were sharp and we executed our clients before they had a chance to complain.

Now I wish make some cutting remarks. How may I to become into the Worshipful Company Barbers? Explain it and send to me the application. I put the stamp for good manners.

Yours friend

[signature]

TOMAS SANTOS

THE WORSHIPFUL COMPANY OF BARBERS

BRIGADIER A F EASTBURN
CLERK

BARBER - SURGEONS' HALL
MONKWELL SQUARE
WOOD STREET
LONDON EC2Y 5BL
TEL: 020-7600 0950
FAX: 020-7606 3857

18 November 2002

Tomas Santos
2 Nevill Gardens
Hove
BN3 7QF

Dear Mr Santos,

Thank you very much for your letter dated 3 November.

You asked for details about becoming a member of the Worshipful Company of Barbers. I should make it clear that we are not in any way a trade association or a fraternity of barbers and hairdressers, although this is where the historical roots lie. Membership of the Company is by invitation rather than application, and your first action should, therefore, be to consult the *City of London Directory and Livery Companies Guide*, which most libraries will have. This book lists members of all Livery Companies and you should see if you know someone who is already a Liveryman in the Barbers' Company and who might be prepared to sponsor you for membership of the Company.

In essence, the Barbers' Company, like most Livery Companies, is primarily a charitable organisation and we look to all our members to make an annual contribution to help with our charitable work. I hope this has answered your queries and wish you well for the future.

Yours sincerely,

A F EASTBURN
CLERK

2 Nevill Gardens
Hove, BN3 7QF

20 November 2002

Brigadier A Feastburn
Clerk to the Worshipful Company of Barbers
Barber-Surgeons' Hall
Monkwell Square
Wood Street
London
EC2Y 5BL

Dear Brigadier Fastburn

Thanks that you had replied my letter.

You describe that I should know 'someone who is already a liveryman' to sponsor me for the membership. I am delighted that I know F J Mallionmbe, Past Master of the Worshipful Company of Butchers. He is a very livery man. Some times is he a bacony man also. Shall I tell him to ring you up?

Yours friend

[signature]

TOMAS SANTOS

THE WORSHIPFUL COMPANY OF BARBERS

BRIGADIER A F EASTBURN
CLERK

BARBER - SURGEONS' HALL
MONKWELL SQUARE
WOOD STREET
LONDON EC2Y 5BL
TEL: 020-7600 0950
FAX: 020-7606 3857

28 November 2002

Tomas Santos
2 Nevill Gardens
Hove
BN3 7QF

Dear Mr Santos,

Thank you for your letter dated 20 November 2002 with the news that you know a Mr Mallion who I note is a Liveryman at the Butchers' Company.

I am sorry if my letter of 18 November was not clear to you but I did emphasise that sponsorship for Admission to the Barbers' Company was by a Liveryman in the Barbers' Company. It follows that Mr Mallion cannot sponsor you for Admission to the Barbers' Company but it is possible that he might know a member of this Company and be happy to effect an introduction to you. Otherwise, I fear, it is back to the *City of London Directory & Livery Companies Guide*.

I am conscious that this may appear less than helpful but I am sure you will understand the need for rules covering the Admission procedures.

Yours sincerely,

A F EASTBURN
CLERK

EMAIL: clerk@barberscompany.org
WEB SITE: www.barberscompany.org

2 Nevill Gardens
Hove, BN3 7QF

4nd December 2002

Brigadier Alan Eastburn
Clerk to the Worshipful Company of Barbers
Barber-Surgeons' Hall
Monkwell Square
Wood Street
London
EC2Y 5BL

Dear Alan

Thank you for yours letter that you said it is 'less than helpful'. You are right again.

It was a fortunate I had not requested 'somethig for the week end' or you should left me completely in the lurch. I hope you cut the hairs with a bit more careful.

I am utterly disaponted to yours feeble performance.

All the best Al.

Yours friend

[signature]

TOMAS SANTOS

TO SPEAK WITH AN OLD

Many old shall muse of nostalgic. He may have a forgettings memory and rankled skin, or skinny bones if he is bent. But be amused of the story of Woolton pie, or Gilbert Harding, or starting handles. He may saying always the same but laugh at him any way.

THE DISCOURSE

Hello you old. How was the world like when you are a little boy?

Is it Monday?

Saturday.

Pardon?

It is the week end, Sir. Now, can you tell to me: what is it like when you were juvenile? Did you travel of the horse, for example?

You must speak more loud, you lad. I have got aids in both my ears.

Are you turned on of the ears trumpet?

What did you said? My canals are full of water. I hear only the rushing cataract.

No, the cataract is of your eye globes, is not it?

Pardon me?

Look I shall increase the noise of your ears instrument. There. Can now you heard me?

Where is my spectacle, boy? All is blur and I see merely clouds.

You have already your lorgnette in your nose.

Och, of hilariously! In due course shall I forgot my head. Tell me, are my tooth at once inside?

Yes, sir, you have all of it. So shall we begin?

Who are you? What do you want of me?

I have some questions. Remember?

Shoot!

When you were boy were there automobiles or must you mount the horse?

Yes.

Were you ride a penny-farting before the auto was discovered?

His name was Dobbin. He was a comely nag.

Did he galloped?

No. We shot him.

Where?

In the twitten.

Whyever?

He caught glanders.

Oh.

And farcy.

Tsk, how shame.

What are we talking about?

You were to tell me of when you were childish.

Oh my, it was a gold age. Our pleasures were easy. I had merely the hoop and stick for a game, or to laugh at the mad in our asylum, or go to the public hanging with cheese sandwiches. Our chicken gave always good eggs, our pigs made bacon, the linnets and pipits and titlarks chanted in the water meadow and my brother worked in the sun shine on the farm.

Was he shepherd?

No. He was small boy so they put him inside the machinery to scavenge of chaff and it cutted his arms off.

Oh, what rotten luck. Had you any sister?

Yes. She went mad of the syphilis and her nose fell off.

Are you sure about that?

We had not penicillin, you see. It was harsh. But jolly.

Where did you lived?

In my house.

Of which town? You have some foreign intonations.

Scotchland. I am a McTavish, native of the Trossachs. Here this book displays of all family tartans pattern. Do you wish to look up my kilt?

No. Time is of the effervescence.

Yes, it is tea time. Will you eat of Dundee cake or drink of a wee glass?

Not just now thanks.

Come son, you are virile; push me around in the gardens. I shall make a circulation in my bath chair and suck my cakes.

The air is a little cooled, sir. Shall you require your shawl or drink some linctus?

I will have wodka in my flask.

Don't be naughty; you are not allowed some alcohols.

You must speak up lad. I cannot hear a word you said; I am completely dead.

Alright then, do your cardigan, Pop.

Oh heaven! I must needs avail of the water closet.

I shall call nurse at once.

Please hurry.

USEFUL SAYINGS TO SPEAK AN OLD

What have you done with your teeths?

Trousers down first, Grandad.

We shall putting you in a home.

PERSONAL OBJECTS VOCABULARY

The electric comb of tooth

The hair rake

The cravat

A shoes

A coat

A cold coat

Your tablets

A CORRESPONDENCE TO THE
FAMUOS ASTROLOGER

2 Nevill Gardens
Hove, BN3 7QF

28nd Febraury 2002

Sir Patrick More, CBE, FRS
'Fartings'
West Street

Dear Sir Patrick

Last night I was look at the prannets with my land lord's stethoscope. He said,
'Can aliens come in England from Uranus?' I know you are screptical so I
explained that you said he more like shall see a white crow.

Will you please answer some my astrological questions?

- What is energy?
- Why it the universe here?
- How big is your trousers?
- Is Uranus a black hole?

Patrick, please send to me a singed photograph.

You are a star.

Yours friend

TOMAS SANTOS
PS. Is a accretion disk too big to went under your xylophone?

SIR PATRICK MOORE CBE FRS

FARTHINGS.
WEST STREET.

TEL:
FAX:
MOB:

Deae Mr. Sanbos,

I am sorry for the delay. Letters mounted up at the BBC, and were not forwarded until now. I am also sorry for bad typing and stamp signature. Problems with my right hand make things difficult. I have done my best!

Energy can be defined as "power of doing work possessed at any instamt by a moving body by virtue of its motion".

Why is the universe here? Frankly, nobody knows.

Can't understand the other two questions, I;m afraid. There is no firm limit to the size of an acceetion disk.

All good wishes

Sincerely

IN THE SURGEON'S OFFICE

The British doctor has the busy sick bay and a lot his patients are dying to visit him. When you go consult a doctor in England do not alarmed if you get a prick with a needle. Certain doctor also in UK are woman, but do not suffer trepidation, merely speak slowly to be understanded.

THE DISCOURSE

Good day surgeon, are you running well?

I am gooding, many thanks. And with you?

Alack, am I indeed out of colour.

Don't again tell me you are queer.

I am so. I fear to my ails. I have an ague. I have the rupture in my collywobbles. My membranes are blown up. I have the flux. I have chopped liver.

My dear patent you are surely the hyperchondriac. Calm you and have some more phlegm. I shall test your regions and put my telescope on you.

Doctor, I have a pain in my bottom's hole. Shall you look into it?

We shall see what we see. How many units drink you?

Very many. Is my digestion corrupt? Do I wrong nerves?

Settle Sir, or must you elevate your blood pressings. I shall check your humours. Bend. Cough! Had you incidentally used the ointment I gaved you?

She tasted as a very poison. Your remedy has gave me the prune-dance.

You must not swallow the medicament inside, you foolish. It should for yours exterior surfaces merely. Are you a pain in the neck?

Yes, the quinsy comes. I have the vapours.

For a curative I shall put this repository.

Not likely! I shall go rub your emolument on my problem. Then we should confer again.

We agree. Tell to my receptionist. She shall appoint you to come back.

I will so, even that she is the impertinent. Let us meet in a long time. God be with you.

Yes.

USEFUL SAYINGS IN THE SURGEON'S OFFICE

I have clenched my head.

I made wind. Will you cup me?

I smoke very much – shall I be cured?

I have suffering of my hip's juncture. Will you leech me?

I am a bag of nevers, Doctor. Am I in a depression?

Will you visited at home? My old man is bent and cannot stand up.

My ear is broken.

I have an ill leg.

DIRECTING A WAY

Very first the things you are probably to have when you are in the UK are to enquire a directions request. Avoid to become lost so precisely require, 'Sir, can you tell me where to go?' He will tell you. Here is the sample dialect.

THE DISCOURSE

Excuse madam. I am a strangler in town and I am get lost. Can you tell where I am?

You are over there, sir.

Well, yes, but will you guide which way I must follow to find the National Palace?

You have somewhat gone round the bend. The National Palace is near Iceland.

No, she is in England.

It's a shop.

Oh, I am fool.

Well sir, you should not begin your quest from this place. You must start elsewhere.

No, I must from this one.

Very well, your expedition is merely a stone's fling of here. Do you notice the zebra crossing?

I see no animals.

No, he is the road safeness utility, with the streaky beacon.

Oh aye, I see his balls oscillating.

Cross there firstly and next walk backwards. Are you understand?

I have you precisely.

Straightly turn and then go away. Where you see a pelican crossing, you must split yourself.

I do not wish the zoo Madam. Cease your menageries.

When the flasher is become green, traverse the way, pass before the traffic lamps by the blacksmith's and the place will be there such that you can't avoid it.

But how if I become completely losed? I shall be in Queer Street.

Merely follow your noise and 'Bob's your ankle'.

Well direction, Madame.

With pleasure.

USEFUL SAYINGS TO ENQUIRE OF YOUR BEARING

Who am I?

This map is the Greek for me.

Bollards!

'Agonistes'
2 Nevill Gardens
Hove, BN3 7QF

3rd Novamber 2002

Brian Lambobe
Director Communications
RNID
19–23 Featherstone Street
London
EC1Y 8SL

Dear Mr Lambobe

Hello. I started to having some problem and I wish yours advice. When I am read the book the black-wobbly floating shapes comes in my visions that I must use the enlargement lens and the big light.

Also, when I was driving my cycle the road became suddenly fuzzy and I struck the milkman with intensity. Many his bottles smashed and the milk fell out. I became bewildered such as blind man's bumf and a car forthwith appeared from nowhere and then it disappeared. Then my road varnished and I plunged in the sea. But with luck I was even alive.

May my eyes be broken? I put the stamp for your important news.

Yours friend

TOMAS SANTOS

RNID ●

for deaf and hard of hearing people

Tomas Santos

2 Neville Gardens
Hove
BN3 7QF

19-23 Featherstone Street
London EC1Y 8SL

Telephone 020 7296 8122
Textphone 020 7296 8122
Fax 020 7296 8035
charlotte.orrell-
jones@rnid.org.uk
www.rnid.org.uk

5 November, 2002

Dear Mr Santos,

Thank you for your letter of 3 November. I was sorry to hear of your problems with your eyes.

Unfortunately, as a charity dealing with deafness, we are unable to offer you any advice or assistance. I suggest that you direct your letter to the RNIB (105 Judd Street, London WC1H 9NE) or seek an appointment with a local optometrist who will be able to help you.

Yours sincerely,

Brian Lamb OBE
Executive Director of Communications

INVESTOR IN PEOPLE

TO RING OF EMERGENCES

It is important to understand to know to ring of police, of fire pompers, or other any emergence. This the correct way.

THE METHOD TO SUMMON OF SUCCOUR

Dial 911 and press button A. You must then follow of instructions:

OPERATOR GIRL: Hello, Emergence. What you want you?
SCARED PERSON: Of ambulace.
OPERATOR GIRL: It comes.
SCARED PERSON: Good bye.
OPERATOR GIRL: Have a nice day.

A CORRESPONDENCE TO THE SPIRITS

2 Nevill Gardens
Hove, BN3 7QF

27rd November 2002

The Leader
Brotherhood Gate Spiritualist Church
21c St James' Street
Brighton
East Sussex

Dear Sir or Madam

I am inquisitive of yours special church and I try to inform my self to the subject Spiritualism. For example, in my nearby convenient store I enquired him if he had the copy *Psychic News* but he said, 'You tell me!' I thought it was not a helping answer to 'pull my legs'.

But you probably knew that already.

May you please send me some informations of your forthcoming talks – if they are not cancelled due to unforeseen circumstances. Or did you already posted them earlier because you 'read my mind'?

Yours friend

TOMAS SANTOS

2 Nevill Gardens
Hove, BN3 7QF

11rd December 2002

The Leader
Brotherhood Gate Spiritualist Church
21c St James' Street
Brighton
East Sussex

Dear Sir or Madam

I had a premonition you wouldn't reply.

TOMAS SANTOS

NATURISM

During thousands years the Anglian people have turned the sod. They have animals of hunting, such that: of pigeons; of badgers; of deers wild; of fishes; and of peasants. So shoot them or enjoy some grass in the country or in the park.

THE DISCOURSE

The sun flickers this morning and there is no currents. Let us wend into the spinney. Will you coming?

It is the champion ruse that would produce a good hunger before ours luncheons. I put the boots.

The sky is mild we may light foot boots or a small coat. No hat will required.

I shall carry my bird glasses.

We are arrived. Ho! What is it there? Is it pond?

It is pond. See there many are some corncrake, swan, fishes and otherwise mammals.

Ach! You are silly ass. That is nary the swan. Squint in my glasses – that is the duck with hers children.

You have reason. It must be here a egg nest. What version is she?

I believe it the mullard: female. Where is the husband?

He gathers, presumably, hunting food to his's kittens.

No, there is the man. He was to bathe his feathers in the cataract.

Shall you sketch him?

I forgot it my Conté pencils. But I shall snap him with my chimera.

Look there by the osiers. Do you see some tits?

Yes, they are female tits. It is a very pleasure. Altogether the birds scream, the bees are fizzling, the waters tickle in the lagoon, and the fowlers smell. It is a natural day.

Oh hang it! We mused and neglect the hour. It is five-and-twenty to two o'clock yet. Ours luncheon should bespoil.

Let us ran home to join our ladies.

Yes, and make one simply enormous lady.

You are the wag.

So you say.

Useful sayings in the outdoors

Cows have been here.

The rain tumbles.

Shall we kill some animals?

Shut the fence!

Bother! A wasp has again bitten on me.

Did a bird fouled on you? That is good chance.

There is much muck here.

Let us home at once.

A CORRESPONDENCE TO THE
FOOTBALL LEG END

2 Nevill Gardens
Hove, BN3 7QF

14nd November 2002

David Beckham
C/o Manchester Untied Football Club
Old Trafford
Manchester
UK

Dear David

Please forgive it that I write you even that you are the known soccer footballer and I am no body particular, but I have the serious question. Here she is:

After a soccer matches how did you get the mud off your balls?

Please send me yours opinions David – *not just the singed picture*. I put the stamp to conserve yours money.

Yours friend

TOMAS SANTOS

MANCHESTER UNITED

IN THE CHURCH

Every one English visits to church of Sundays. The Church England (Anglian Church) has spread his testicles around a globe, to Africa, Asia, USA and not Ireland. In winter English church are freezers. Put the coat.

THE DISCOURSE

God morning Reverend Father. I am newly to yours church and I wished to met you.

Welcome in our congregation then.

Your church indeed is vivacious, Vicar; your temples are bulging.

Yes, my congregations are swollen. What thought you of us?

I was impressed such that your singing was without musical accomplishment.

You are nice to point it; I rest on my choristers.

They are gay.

Yes, they scream well the hymnal. What thought you of Miss Jibbens on my organ?

She plays with spunk, Vicar. I shall remember her in my prayers.

I hope also you shall remember those that are sick of our church.

I shall made donation in your sick bowl, Vicar.

Will you join ours prayer club? Our ladies have cast off

clothing of every kind to raise moneys. Will you examine them in the vestry?

I will come in my best trousers.

Shall I put your sister in the club also?

I have the worry she shall not like it, Vicar.

Worry will kill you – let our church help.

Very well. Should I set on fire a tapir?

Not really, merely visit in ours service on Easter and lay an egg on the tabernacle.

I look forward it. God bless Vicar.

God bless.

USEFUL SAYINGS FOR THE CHURCH

Tell your prayers.

Tell grace.

Have you the surplus surplice?

Hassocks.

Cassocks.

Evensnog.

Happy-clappy.

The church is kept locked at all times.

A CORRESPONDENCE TO A ARCHBISHOB

2 Nevill Gardens
Hove, BN3 7QF

3nd August 2002

Dr George Caries
Archbishop of Canterbury Tales
Lambeth Palace
London
SE1 7JU

Dear George

Hello. I hope you will forgive me to be informally but the Apostlers did not called Jesus 'Archbishop Jesus', they referred to him only 'Jesus'.

I heard that you shall soon retired to be the Archbishop of Canterbury and all the other priests are fight to be the next one Archbishop. One them has got a beard so I don't think he is very good one. Perhaps he growed it if he was scared to look as the *woman* because all those dresses you wear.

Anyway, here's some questions:

- What is yours favorite hymn?
- What is you hobby (do you fancy pigeons?)
- How can I kissed your ring?

Please sent me a singed photograph with your dress on.

God bless you George.

Yours friend

TOMAS SANTOS

2 Nevill Gardens
Hove, BN3 7QF

1th November 2002

Dr George Caries
Archbishob Canterbury
Lambeth Palace
London
SE1 7JU

Dear Archbishop

I was in England before and I had posted the letter to you with some the question. But I went suddenly in my home land for my mother became unwell when a donkey bit on her legs and she got severe ass bruises. But now she is again well and I am again here. Thank Christ!

Now look here: my land lord told me you had not replied from my letter and moreover is it *nine moths*. I turn my another cheek and I put *again* the stamp that you may now respond. Or have you thieved my postage?

I should wish very much you may sent the singed photo. Don't send one of you because you are out of date. Send one of the new one Archbishop of the Anglian Communion – the man with the long scratchy beard who is a hairy primate.

If this impossible may you please return of my stamps? They quite expensive.

God Bless

Yours extremely obedient friend

TOMAS SANTOS

Mr Tomas Santos
2 Nevill Gardens
Hove
BN3 7QF

Miss Sarah Benson
Secretary to the Revd Canon Dr David Marshall
Chaplain to the Archbishop of Canterbury

6 November 2002

Dear Mr Santos,

Thank you very much for your letter to the Archbishop dated 1 November.

Sadly, it seems that your previous letter never arrived here at Lambeth Palace, for we keep copies of all our correspondence and do not have a copy of the letter on record.

At present we are in a period of interregnum, whereby there is currently no Archbishop of Canterbury - Dr George Carey has recently retired and Dr Rowan Williams will not be enthroned as his successor until February next year. We are therefore unable to send you an autographed photograph at this time, but will certainly keep your request on file and will send you a signed photograph of Dr Rowan Williams as soon as possible on his arrival here at Lambeth Palace.

With all good wishes,

Yours sincerely,

Sarah Benson

2 Nevill Gardens
Hove, BN3 7QF

2rd April 2003

Miss Sarah Benson
Secretay to the Revd Canon Dr David Marshall, Chaplain to the Archbishop of
Canterbury
Lambeth Place
London
SE1 7JU

Dear Miss Benson

I received it yours letter 6rd November 2002 to explained such that it is a 'period interregnum'. But Dr Willaims now is on the throne and I anticipate your announcement that you will send me the singed photograph 'as soon possible'.

I am getting bit nervous. You have my stamps before. Shall you soon send me? Or what is gong on?

God Bless Sarah

Yours friend

TOMAS SANTOS

LAMBETH PALACE

Mr Tomas Santos
2 Nevill Gardens
Hove
BN3 7QF

Abigail Clausen
Clerical Assistant

22 April 2003

Dear Mr Santos

Thank you very much for your letter to the Archbishop dated 1 November 2002 requesting he sends you an autographed photograph for your collection.

The Archbishop is delighted to send you the enclosed personally autographed photograph, and this comes with his very warm regards.

With all good wishes,

Abigail Clausen

WITH THE TAILOR

UK persons look ever sleek in their refinery. A tailor in UK shall never used machinery that tears your suit – he will do it by hand. They are fast also and will stitch you up before you knew what happened. So put your new doublet and spats, and ponce around town.

THE DISCOURSE

Hello tailor.

It is fine to see you, sir.

I require some altering my costume. Can you increase the tension in my home or must I drop my trousers for a proper seeing to?

With willing, sir. What is amiss your garment?

I have a discomfort in my fundament; I required more allowance. Check my pants if something is wrong.

Discard your pants and I shall correct him tomorrow.

But I must had some trouser to wear in a jiffy. Shall you measure me?

I can do you on Thursday.

But I am hasty. I should not wander in the city without trouser. You must execute me in an extremely soon moment.

Very well. Will you have a fit upstairs?

Can it not here? I shall remove my singlet and have a fit in my pants.

OK then, let's have it off and I will discover how big you are in the vestibule.

Ouch! What did you? I felt a prick in my bottom.

Forgive it sir. I needled you and penetrated you erroneously.

Blow me! Show me your pattern without delay then I must suddenly went shopping.

Come again in this afternoon and you should had the suite in a stripes fashion.

Have you gone crazy? I should look as a popinjay.

Perhaps then the herring-tweed with a Prince of Wails Check?

That is a excellent idea; I am over the moon. I shall come again back.

Yes, why don't you go away?

USEFUL SAYINGS IN THE TAILOR

These pants make my wife hot. Please be suggestive.

Coat me!

I wish purchase a brasserie for the medium woman.

Can you make me a coat from my own skin?

My sister requires the loose costume for street walking.

Belt me!

Sock me!

Boot me!

Fleece me!

Is my shit hanging out?

A CORRESPONDENCE TO THE ACTRESS

2 Nevill Gardens
Hove, BN3 7QF

7rd November 2002

Ewan MacGregor
C/o PDQ
Dreary House
34–43 Russell Street
London
WC2B 5HA

Dear Ewan

Yesterday I came in my best trousers to see you staring in a film, *Moulin Rogue!* I saw you before in the another one film, *Rouge Trader* and yours acting was excellent. But you speak the dialogs such as greased lighting so my land lord daughter transladed the words on my thigh with his finger in the darkness, such that I should understand the meanings.

Ewan, you are the Renaissance man; yours acting is laughable but also you can pretend be serous, so I shall proposition you: I had started the acting group in Brighton that we visit in the hospitals to act funny and do the patients. Ours group is called 'Laughing Gas' so we have the stand-up joke man (rudely) and the puppet man that all his arms fall off (hilarous!).

But all hospitals are wary to employed us so we wish the patron to distract attention or raised the profile. Will you it? It should be the charty work and we can made you the salary £11. Then we shall put yours picture and yours endrosements on ours pubelicity and everyone should want us. I require the precise letter to said yes so please don't not merely send the singed photograph – *that's what David Beckham did.*

I give you my wishes that we shall soon 'cooking with gas'.

May the forks be with you!

Yours friend

TOMAS SANTOS

Photo Sarah Dunn

A BREAKFAST

The completely English breakfast famous is the entire world.
You must prove it at once and gobble him. Delicious.

THE DISCOURSE

Good morning land lady.

And so. What you your breakfast?

I should bacons; the egg; put bread fire; beans cooked with
the furnace; toast; dark cakes; coffee; juice of orang, and
biscuits.

Do you take the sausage?

You put your finger on it.

I have also toadstools, will you like that?

I should eat abundance they.

I hope I shall pleasure you.

Indeed, I have a hunger.

I will cook thems forthwith.

Yes ma'am.

USEFUL SAYINGS OF BREAKFAST

Toast me.

Marmalade solders.

I have jammed my fingers.

Scrambled ovaries.

A CORRESPONDENCE TO THE
MASTER OF THE ROLES

2 Nevill Gardens
Hove, East Sussex
BN3 7QF

113th May 2005

The Master of the Rolls, the Right Hon. the Lord Phillips of Worth Matravers
C/o Brooks's Club
60 St James's Street
London
SW1A 1LN

Dear Master

I am visiting in England since a short time to made study in the language college and English history. In my home land we have not a Master of the Rolls. It is the good idea and I have some question for you.

Can I please have:

- Two cheese and tomato on brown with poopy seeds
- One 'Chutney Surprise' on the crusty knot roll
- One spicy chicken tikka bap. *No lime pickle*

Just put it on the bill. (I included the envelope for invoicings.)

I think you the best thing since sliced beard!

Yours friend

TOMAS SANTOS

IN THE ORCHESTRA CONCERT

UK has many musicals such that *The Prannets* by Gustav Holst. To visit in the concert you may hear wonderful musics when you sit down on your orchestra stalls. So if the bus conductor comes of the stage to wave his arms in the *Air on a G String*, applause him.

THE DISCOURSE

What will we listen tonight, Wilfred? I am forgotten.

Here, see the menu, Violet. It will be firstly Flight of the Bumble Wasp, *then* Ride the Valkyries *by Robert Wagner, followed of Handel's* Large.

What becomes after the intromission?

Well, they will do for Haydn's strumpet concerto and finish off Beethoven's Erotica.

At home I am exploring Wagner's *Ring.*

That sounds horrible.

It is sixteen hours but I like to listen it.

Did you know of English composer Henry Purcell?

I know only his opera *Dildo and Aeneas* conducted of Benjamin Britten.

Do you like The Fairy Queen?

Yes, he is a good conductor.

What of that Miss A Brevis?

Never heard of her.

Look Violet, I have not before asked of you, do you perform of the music insurment?

Piano is my forte.

How very lovely.

Shall I give you a little snatch in my apartment subsequently?

You're telling me! Did you know I tooted a wind when I was at school in Broadstairs?

That interesting, Wilfred.

Yes, we boys made the lucky drip for our instruments and I got the horn. But I could not well blow myself and I didn't stand up to examination with the other ones.

Did you matriculate?

We all matriculated together, in Sandwich.

I can't believe me.

Yus. But I came last because I can don't read music notes. Unhappily I am delinquent of ability.

But I have heard you titillate the ivories, with cross hands.

I was jamming.

You must have a very good ear.

Pardon?

I said: you must have a very good ears.

No. I can't tell my Arne from my Elgar.

Aha! Here comes Sir Rattle now. It is Elgar's *Enema Variations.*
I hope he will get a warm hand on his opening.

Let us give him the clap.

He deserves it.

USEFUL SAYINGS IN THE MUSICAL CONCERT

Bravo!

Andante molto.

Encore.

When's the interval?

MUSIC INSTRUMENTS VOCABULARY

Piano

The oud

Aluminium whistle keychain

Congalongs

Chocolate éclair

Viola of the knees

A CORRESPONDENCE TO THE BEETLE HELPER

Top Flat
2 Nevill Gardens
Hove, East Sussex
BN3 7QF

11rd May 2005

Sir George Martin, Kt, CBE
C/o The College of Arms
Queen Victoria Street
London
EC4V 4BT

Dear Sir George

You are the excellent producer that you made the arrangemences to The Beetles songs of John Lemon and Paul McCartney, Bingo Star, and the other one. In the 'Swingeing Sixties' you produced: *I Want to Hold Your Ham, Eleanor ~~Roosevelt~~ Rigby, When I'm 604,* and *We All Lived in a Yellow Submersible.*

The College of Arms told me that you have new arms. Didn't you have arms before? Or did they fell off with old age?

Your new arms are:

Arms: Azure on a Fess nebuly Argent between three Stag Beetles Or five Barrulets Sable.
Crest: On a wreath Argent and Azure A House Martin proper holding under the sinister wing a Recorder in bend sinister mouthpiece downwards Or.
Motto: AMORE SOLUM OPUS EST
Badge: A Zebra statant proper supporting with the dexter foreleg over the shoulder an Abbot's Crozier Or.

In my Latin book your motto means 'Love only is work' and I could agree more. What is a Fess nebuly Argent?

Your admirable friend

TOMAS SANTOS
Quid quid latine dictum sit, altum videtur

AIR STUDIOS
Lyndhurst Hall
Lyndhurst Road
Hampstead
London
NW3 5NG

Tomas Santos, Esq.,
Top Flat,
2 Nevill Gardens,
Hove, East Sussex,
BN3 7QF

13th June 2005

Dear Mr. Santos,

Your letter has been sent to me from the College of Arms and I see that you are puzzled by the ancient words that are used in heraldry. The arms are stated as "Azure on a Fess nebuly Argent". This means that it is blue background on the upper part of the shield on a "Fess", which is a horizontal line dividing the shield into two. "Nebuli Argent" means silver, cloud like. In other words, wavy. It goes on.... "between three Stag Beetles Or, which indicate gold beetles. "Five Barrulets Sable"... This is five straight horizontal lines together in dark or black. These five lines represent the lines on a musical stave.

My motto "Amore Solum Opus Est" can be interpreted the way you have said, but a freer translation which is the one I meant, is that love only is needed.

Kindest regards.

I am sure you know what that means.

Sir George Martin, CBE

Best wishes & Tomas

TO SPEAK WITH CHILDRENS

The childrens are same in the world. The laughter and behaviour with unmade of the hairs. You should do amusing conversation with some rascal in order improved your linguistic capacities.

THE DISCOURSE

Come child, do not be childish. Do not mud my floors.

I wish play, Mama.

Very well nipper, but do not select your nose. Be well-bread – you must stroke your tooth and rake your hairs.

Must I polish the face?

Indeed. And give to your greatmother the kissing.

No, she is like the horse's end.

You are scallywag. Not employ this tonality of the tongue with my! How the challenge you speak me such that? Regard your elder and improve them. I shall slipper you. You must be trounced.

Very well, Mother, I am now corrected.

A good boy.

USEFUL SAYINGS TO CHILDRENS

Sit you and shut of mouth.
Golly gumdrops!

You are no good and will amount to nothing.
Cleanse the shoes.
Attention-deficit hyperactivity disorder.
Who has blown off?

PASSTIME VOCABULARY

Horses ridding
Wrestlers
Stamps acquision
Music
Digging
Macráme
Ferrets
Balling
Anus

A CORRESPONDENCE TO THE BOOKMAKERS

2 Nevill Gardens
Hove, BN3 7QF

20rd October 2002

Children Book Editor
Puffin Books
80 Strand
London
WC2R 0RL

Dear Madame

In my home land was it such that I begun the storey for childrens. In the moment I had completed to translated this book with the character is called Shag the pony. He made some funny adventure in the farmsyard. I had put the sample on the another page that you shall read him. (The song should have actions!)

I think this should be the poplar book.

Yours friend

TOMAS SANTOS

Enclosed: excellent sample

Shag the pony. Part 1.

In the farmsyard stands the cow, the pig, the ass and the dogs. The sun is shining in the farm such that all are happy animals. Suddenly out came the pony. His name was Shag the pony. He had made the first prize in the pony show that they all gave him the clap to celebrate his winnings. Mary the Cow gave him a special pat on the back. 'Three cheers to Shag!' she bellows. Then all the animals friends chanted the special song.

Shag the pony, Shag the pony
Shag Shag Shag
Shag the pony, Shag the pony
His tail wag
Shag the pony, Shag the pony
Big nose-bag
Shag the pony, Shag the pony
Shag Shag Shag!

PUFFIN

80 Strand, London WC2R ORL
Telephone: 020 7010 3000 Fax: 020 7010 6691
www.puffin.co.uk

Thank you for sending your work for our consideration. We regret that out lists are very full and we are no longer accepting unsolicited manuscripts.

We enclose a separate sheet with information which you may find useful.

In the meantime we wish you success in placing your work elsewhere and are sorry that Penguin Children's Books cannot help you further.

Whilst every reasonable care will be taken on manuscripts, we cannot be held responsible for any loss or damage.

ROMANCE

In England is the art of chivalry. Every man must make
always the compliment of a lady and hold for her the doors,
stand when she comes, buy some rich presents, and guard
her from wolfs. If she asked: 'Darling, do you liked my new
frock?', the man *must* said yes or it will a terrible evening and
recrimination. To learn amorous vocabulary, here are some
dialogue. (Note: A gentleman must rise always his hat before
he strikes a lady.)

THE DISCOURSE

I love to you, Olive.

I love to you also, Quentin.

You have a beautiful tooth.

Thank you.

As well you have a beautiful leg.

Just the one?

And the beautiful black hairs.

On my leg?

They tumble on you shoulder.

None on my head then.

Olive!

What?

Did anyone told you have some provocative eyes?

*You make overdone the adulation, Quentin. Cease now of
your compliments.*

But I want to give you one.

Flattery are better to be more few. You try too much hard.

But Olive, you have a lovely chest and your neck looks like a goose.

You mean a swan.

Yes. I shall give you a pearl necklace.

OK, enough already. You are hot and brothered. Stop now or I must slap your bottom.

You're making it worse. I am overcame of desires. I am hypnotized by your nose.

Really?

A man should give a millions dollars to kiss on such a nose.

If I had a million for this nose I'd blow it on myself.

You deserved it. Your waste is narrow, your pelvic griddle is slender, your belly is fair, and your figure is slime.

No, I must be more slimmer. I have too much fat thighs.

Scribble and balderdash! You are very gorgeous.

Thighs apart, you mean.

No. I do not love either completely skinny or fatty legs.

You prefer something in between?

Yes.

You indeed know how to made a lady feel, Quentin. I am week of the knees. Come in my bed at once.

Must I take of my pants?

Well, you can not eat of the chocolate with a wrapping on him.

OK, I am ready.

Oh, to goodness' sake. You look an absurd to be in only your balaclava.

I will have it off forthwith.

I thought that was the general idea.

Move you over then, Olive.

Oh blimey Quentin, you are more bristles than which you look.

Quiet woman. It is bad conduct to speak with the mouth full up.

USEFUL PHRASES FOR THE ROMANCE

May I steal a kiss?

Sir, I wish marry your daughter's hand.

Stop yer ticklin', Jock.

These johnnies are past their use-by date.

TO WRITING LETTERS

You must have always the stiff udder lip in England but also must you made mannerly on yours letters. Here are a example for example.

THE EXSAMPLE LETTER

My Darling Sir,

I have received yours delivery of the 14rd inst to hand. I should like point out such that you made mistake to send me ~~two mongoose two mongooses two mongeese~~ a mongoose and another one with it. I put them back in your packet and return it herewithe. Kindly removed me now of yours annoying list.

I remain, Sir, your most obedient sweetheart,

A CORRESPONDENCE TO THE
ANOTHER ARCH BISHOP

Top flat
2 Neville Gardens
Hove
East Sussex
BN3 7QF
England
Untied Kingdom
of Great Britain
(and North Ireland)

13rd April 2005

Dr Most Rev. Seán Brady, DCL, (Roman Catholic) Archbishop of Armagh,
Chairman of the Irish Episcopal Conference, and (Roman Catholic) Primate of All
Iceland
Ara Coeli
Armagh
BT61 7QY

Dear Most Reverend Doctor Archbishop Primate Chairman

I am again in England since I made 'the time off' in my English studies to did the
visit in some countries. But I now am back – like the prodigal song. I have put some
my travel photos for you. Please return it if you browsed on them. When I came back
in England my land lord's daughter told me such that the 'New Pope' is now in his
office. I did not pick it up these momentous information last week because I was
being ill on the boat.

The main points is: I wish now congratulate to Pope Benedict XIV (16th) but I have
not the suitable contacts detail. I know he lives in the Vatican City but I do not know
what house or the street. Can you send to me the correct numbers? As quick as
possibly, if you don't mind.

I will jump of joy if you will. I look forward to you.

Yours friend

TOMAS SANTOS

PS. Don't forget my photos.

Ara Coeli, Cathedral Road
Armagh BT61 7QY

Telephone 028 3752 2045
Fax   028 3752 6182
             (Country Code 44)

Email admin@aracoeli.com
www.armagharchdiocese.org

May 18, 2005

Mr Tomas SANTOS
Top Flat
2 Neville Gardens
HOVE
East Sussex
BN3 7QF

Dear Mr Santos

Thank you for your recent letter. I am glad to hear that you enjoyed your trip.

The details you require to contact the Holy Father are as follows:

His Holiness Pope Benedict XVI
Vatican City
Europe

I am also returning your photos. Thank you for letting me see them.

With every good wish,

Yours sincerely,

+ Seá Brady

Archbishop of Armagh

ON AN AIRPORT

All traveller must go in the airports. If you need informations you shall find the airport staff are all over the place. So prepare these discourse and then you can just go away.

THE DISCOURSE

Hello Miss. I am arrived in your terminal but I must know some knowledge of where I am go. Are you an enquiring person?

You must ask of our informations. They will tell you where to go – they have a reputation for it. Here comes a somebody. She shall make you trip good.

Oh, hello lady, may I probe you?

I am runaway information. What do you want?

I wish to go away.

Go on then, I'm not stopping you.

No, you must tell me: is yet my fly open?

Which number fly is you?

Here, see on my billet. I go to Prussia at half to 9 clock.

Ah, you have the low-cut airline. It is not now time to get board.

When may I get board?

In a half an hour they undo the plane. You must made the connective bus in our number 2 terminal. They will take you for a complete ride.

Where shall I leave them?

Talk to the diver and he will tell you where to get off. Do you have a case to put?

Yes. I put two suits cases and a handbag.

You must check the baggages forthwith.

I think I will urinate myself first. Where is the rest rooms?

Next to Starbucks.

I am about to go.

Have a nice day.

Hello, are you the bag man?

Good day, Sir. May I see you pass port at this time?

I have come of your another terminal.

Did you packed your own privates?

Yes.

Do you have gas?

Pardon?

Have you: knifes; gas cookers; killing gun; nail flies; exploding bombs; scissor; electric apparatus, or water?

Not really.

Fruit?

Pardon me?

Have you fruit?

I have quinces.

Eat them. Have you visited in farms?

I went in the zoological gardens.

You may pass to the baggages check-in at this time.

I see.

Have a beautiful vacation.

Well met, check-in lady. Here are my baggage.

Complete the luggage label and I will tell you where you can stick it.

There. It is done.

You now are lovely and may pass out in the flying sector.

Bye.

Hello, man. It is a pleasant day.

Passport.

Here she is, friend.

Come on, I haven't got all day. Walk inside that inspection machine. Put your heavy metals on the drawer. They wish radiograph your handbag.

Thanks heaven. I made no alarum to ring. Am I clarified?

Yes. Go now in the antechamber. You may purchase tax-free gods beside the fountain.

I shall drop in. Thank you buddy.

USEFUL SAYINGS OF THE AIRPORT

Fatten your seat belt.

This your capitain speaking. We soon will crash in London so sit and relax you.

Do not rub me up the wrong way, lady, my dander is up.

I wish speak Stelios!

A CORRESPONDENCE TO THE PLANE SPOTTERS

Top flat
2 Nevill Gardens
Hove, BN3 7QF

11rd October 2002

The Director
Recruitment Section
Notional Air Traffic Control Services Ltd
1 Kemble Street
London
WC2B 4AP

Dear Sir

I am visiting in UK since a year to study the English perfect. I now speak very well such that I wish to apply at NATCS to become the airs traffic controller. I can now spoke well English, also I have the enthusism.

Do not alarmed that I suffer the narcolepsy if I forgot my pills. I very often do not suddenly go asleep (and I wake again up quite soon). Another person usually helped me awake up.

I shall coming in Kemble Street on next Tuesday for the interview. I hope this convenient. Tell me what the good time.

'Fingers crosed'.

Sincerely yours friend

TOMAS SANTOS

PS. Please send me the map. I am terrible with a directions.

HR SERVICES – Recruitment and Selection
National Air Traffic Services Ltd, T12, One Kemble Street, London WC2B 4AP
Telephone: (01489) 612157
E-mail: hr.servicesrecruitment@nats.co.uk

PERSONAL
22nd October 2002

Mr T Santos
Top Flat
2 Nevill Gardens
Hove
BN3 7QF

Dear Tomas

TRAINEE AIR TRAFFIC CONTROL – RECRUITMENT

I am writing further to your recent letter dated 11th October 2002 regarding the above-mentioned position.

I am sorry to have to tell you that I have been advised by our Medical Department that because of your condition you would be outside the standard required in order to obtain a Class One Medical Certificate to enable you to become a Trainee Air Traffic Controller. Therefore, I am unable to continue further with your application.

I realise that this must come as a disappointment to you but I would like to thank you for the interest in the Company.

Yours sincerely

Ruth Wallace
Recruitment Adviser
Room T1213
Tel: 020 7832 6651
Fax: 020 7832 6633
e-mail: ruth.wallace@nats.co.uk

AT THE POSTAGE OFFICE

The postage office may be a meeting plaice of the village. Go there for the pictures card or to bought elasticated bands. You can make fun with the elder peoples of arthritic when you buy your stamps, and then you can lick them.

THE DISCOURSE

Good day my man.

Cashier number 5 please.

The weather are rather fine.

Cashier number 2 please.

Do you speak English?

Very Sir. How shall I help to you?

I beg you?

What do you want exactly?

I must telegraph and I wish send things but I should pick your brians for I believe my packet is too large.

Put him in the balance.

Here is he.

Cashier number 5 please.

What balance does my packet make?

He weighs median, Sir. I can handle him with pleasure.

What expenditure shall it?

Where you like your things to go? We will send them in every direction.

In Europe.

Very good. He will amount to seven guineas for air deliverance.

Do it!

You first must nominate your fillings.

They are English gewgaws.

Just fill in this form and I will service that lady behind.

No, I want more. My French letter is a funny shape. Can you stamp on it correctly?

Sir, our stampings contraption uses the latest methodism.

Very good. I am certain it shall travel with celerity.

Cashier number 5 please.

Here now is my complete form. What should I do?

Stick it!

All is now done. May I push my packet in your hole?

Yes.

Until we meet again then.

Nope, they are close us down.

Cheers mate.

USEFUL SAYINGS OF THE POSTAGE ORIFICE

Can you envelope me?

Please lick my gums.

Ribbon me.

I wish to transmit a post.

A CORRESPONDENCE TO THE LIGUIST

2 Nevill Gardens
Hove, BN3 7QF
United Kingdom of Great Britain (& North[ern] Ireland)

18st February 2003

Noam Chomsky
Institute Professor; Professor of Linguistics, Linguistic Theory, Syntax, Semantics,
Philosophy of Language
MIT Linguistics and Philosophy
77 Massachusetts Avenue Bldg. E39-219
Cambridge, MA 02139
USA

Dear Professor Chomsky

I read many the language book and including yours indispendable treatises with
notions of language meanings. I think English is the hard one language to made
properly syntax or truly the meaning. Should you agreed? For the example are some
news paper 'headlines' such that I had gathered him. These are beneath you:

- **DOG CHEWED MAYOR'S TESTIMONIALS**
- **WOMAN KICKED BY HUSBAND SAID TO BE GREATLY IMPROVED**
- **MACARTHUR FLIES BACK TO FRONT** (Second Word War)
- **DR FUCHS OFF TO SOUTH ICE** (Sir Vivian Fuchs was the English prospector)
- **MAN HELD OVER PROSTITUTES**
- **FRENCH PUSH BOTTLES UP GERMAN REAR** (Second World War)
- **CHICHESTER CONQUERS THE HORN** (Round the world boat man)
- **DR FUCHS OFF AGAIN!**

Professor, Shall you accepted if I proposition you to become Patron to my new
group: Grammars Accelerated Simplifaction Panel (GASP)? Then can we sort
everything out to made English quite more simple. We should pay you the salary £7
and you shall just do some lectures (merely five or six every months). I put $5 such
that it shall allow to pay your responding mail.

All the best Norm.

Yours friend

TOMAS SANTOS

PS: Did you aware that yours name is the anagarm to 'Moan'?

MASSACHUSETTS INSTITUTE OF TECHNOLOGY

E39-219
Department of Linguistics and Philosophy
Cambridge, Massachusetts 02139

March 10, 2003

Dear Tomas Santos,

Interested to hear about GASP. Can only wish you all the luck in the world -- but from afar, I'm afraid. Can't accept the gift. My tax bracket is too high.

Sincerely,

Noam Chomsky

IN THE GREENGROCER'S

At every street in UK are the cheerful greengrocer's with his brown paper bag, his jolly costermongers song, his cauliflower ear, and his wrong apostrophe. 'Buy my goosegog's; the'yre lovey!' he scream's all day – it is in his marrow. Follow this discourse to get serviced with a fruit.

THE DISCOURSE

Good morrow. Are you a fruit shopkeeper?

Yes, Sir. What may I do you for?

Are you also a vegetable man?

Yes. I am a fruit and a vegetable.

Tell me then, what available you?

I have: vine peache's; huckleberrie's; egg fruit; pomme-pomme's; grapefruit's; mango's; melon's, and today we have also mulberrie's.

Do you go round the mulberry bush?

No. We have the fruit,s collection of Nine Elm's and I daily exhibition them in pleasing heaps'.

You have handsome plum's my dear fellow.

They are tasty, isn't it.

What of your rhubub's? Are them good of growth?

Yes, Sir. They is ready to eat! We put the horses manure on it.

I put custard on mine.

Deliciously.

Your raspberrie's bouquet is sweet indeed, with an exquisite nose.

Pick your own.

Tell me, what are they exotic fruit's your sales clerk's have?

They are ugli.

No. One of they is an pretty girl. Surely she has nice melon's.

Did you seen her juicy pear?

They are ripe, in my judgment.

Please not squeeze them. The skin become's with smudge's of customer finger.

Say, buddy, have you good lemon's?

Are you taking the pith?

I require merely her juices.

Well then, they lemon's are that for which you are looking. They is saturated and will excrete their's elixir with ease. My father also and I make a gurgle with the fluid for the hurtful throat's.

How are your Granny Smith?

Hard.

What about your Cox?

This year they are rotted and shrivellated of a hot summer.

Cor.

Drat it, Sir. You elbowed my arrangement's and my bloody orange's are tumbled of the pavement.

You have unstable piles, O testy costermonger.

I suppose you think your'e funny.

Tell me jolly green grocer, what of your vegetable's?

We have the usual: zucchinis'; plantain's; pimientos'; yam's; celeriac; tomatois; potatos; artichoke's global and artichoke's Jerusalem.

You have them all of memory, my good merchant?

You think I dont know my onion's?

Do you squash or sprout?

They is not came of this month. The frost had blasted them. Any else?

Have you some cheap roots to made a cheesy vegetable soup?

My swedes are going for a snog.

I need a leek. And a *long* one.

I have a whopper. Let me put it in your sack. Will you take my pulses?

Never. The bean procures me flatus and I always take a pea in the tin can.

Oh.

But I need some okra for make my especial curry. Have you it?

Sir, I have ladies fingers in my back passage. Shall I retrieve you some them?

No.

Goodbye.

Goodbye darling.

Useful saying's in the greengrocer's

Iv'e got a lovely bunch of coconut's.
When can I have a banana again?
An apple for the teacher.
Cherry ripe, cherry ripe.
Orange's and lemon's.
Strange fruit.

A CORRESPONDENCE TO A BREAD WEIGHER

Top Flat
2 Nevill Gardens
Hove, East Sussex
BN3 7QF

16nd May 2005

The Bread Weigher
Alcester Town Hall
Henley Street
Alcester
Warwickshire
B49 5QX

Dear Bread Weigher

I am visiting in England since a short while to study in the language college and to English history. May you explain me what is the purpose the ancient office of the Bread Weigher? For example, how much often do you weigh the bread? Do you use your loaf to add up of the sums?

I noticed there is other ones unusural jobs in Alcester: Fish Taster, Flesh Taster, Ale Taster (that one must popular!), Searcher and Sealer of Leather (what that for?), and Brook Looker. Will the Brook Looker look in the brooks or try look for the brooks, or will merely he look at the brooks all day? What is he looking? It must be bit boring. Maybe that you could downsized e.g. the Ale Taster became also the Brook Looker so you joined the dreary job with the more nice one job? You can use this idea if you liked.

Yours friend

TOMAS SANTOS

PS. Do you drive the Rolls?

Court Leet and Court Baron of the
Most Honourable Henry Jocelyn Seymour,
Marquess of Hertford

Senor Santos,

I hope you are enjoying your sojourn in England, and that your studies are going well. Will you be here for the Trafalgar Day Bicentenary celebrations in October.

Tomas, do you know I was similarly flabbergasted at being elected as bread-weigher for the old and ancient manor of Alcester. I accepted because I needed the dough, but found there was none to be had, not even a stipend.

My purpose is to determine with regard to the price of wheat the proper weight of loaves offered for sale within the manor, ensuring it fair, the texture to be good and wholesome.
This particular process takes around eight hours per year, but in common with the modern day weights and measures council appointment justifies twelve months of employment. This is handsomely covered of course by the three and a half billion pound rebate which we claim from our friends in the EEC.

The brook-looker looks first for the brooks, then in the brooks, then at the brooks. The order being of paramount concern. Be assured that this position is neither dreary nor boring, and is carried out with the utmost sobriety. Indeed the confluence of the rivers Alne and Arrow have the most babbling brooks in bard county.

Downsizing is an Americanism which would be frowned upon by the steward of the manor. Ale tasting and brook looking are distinctly separate. "We have always done it that way". Probably because babbling brooks combined with our babbling ale tasters and their babbling court leet entourage would be so cacophonous in nature as to disturb the peace of the good citizens of Alcester.

I am flattered that as the humble bread-weigher of the court you have selected myself as your correspondent. It has prompted me to consider a fan club, and you Tomas, as its inaugural member, could represent me.
Is there a demand for men in frocks in the Brighton and Hove area?

I have no photograph as this is such a modern media, but I have commissioned a local artist to paint my portrait.

Buenos Dias,

Andy Mills
Bread Weigher

Top Flat
2 Nevill Gardens
Hove, East Sussex
BN3 7QF

2rd June 2005

Mr Andy Mills
The Beard Weigher
C/o Court Leet and Court Baron of the Most Honourable Henry Jocelyn
Seymour, Marquess of Hertford
Alcester Town Hall
Alcester
Warwickshire
B49 5QX

Dear Mr Mills

Crumbs! It is quite a lot surprise such that you have a so much revelant name.
For the mills made the flours then Mr Mills weighed the bread. I propose a toast.

I am a lot fluttered that you wish I became the inaugural member to the Bread
Weigher's Fans Club – you are butter me up. But I have the few questions.

1. Shall I get the costume (the black dress and livery stripes), such as you?
2. Must there be long meetings?
C. Shall we eat the bread only or can we had some crisps?
5. Will ladies came or do you prefer male members?

I don't wish sound crusty but there is a lot much to organised.

Perhabs we could ask the College of Arms to made us the full accomplishment
arms: with the Baps Argent between Buns statant proper holding a Sliced
Wholemeal volant in bend sinister. What did you think?

I am pleased that you are commissioned the artist to done your self-portrait.
Make sure he doesn't paint your nose too big.

Yours friend

TOMAS SANTOS, BWFC

IN THE HOSTEL

To visit in the another land must you ever settle in the hostel or sleep in the other man's bed. This discourse should help to you to manage speak.

THE DISCOURSE

Good morning man. I wish some remarks for the director hotel.

Sir, I am at your dispersal.

I left my values here last night but my pass book is vanished. I probed your mistress but she was a rude.

If you think she's rude you should meet our Complaints girl.

Will you discount me, then?

Sir, I discount you already.

We improve directly. Now then, also is my bidet broken and I cannot got News 24.

If yours bidet is wrong your chambermaid will look into it. Or must I come up there?

I will take advantage of the chambermaid.

Is there more?

Yes. I wish take my tomorrow breakfast from a waitress in my bed.

Very well. Would you like us to alarm you?

Yes. One furthermore question please.

What?

There is a widow in my shower.

And?

I cannot shut her up.

I see.

She is frigid.

Do you refer the French widow, Sir?

No, the French widow is in my bed room. Her opening is first class. The other is old and stiff and is letting always a terrible wind. She made the gooses bumps on my person and I cannot stick it out any longer.

I shall ask our man to investigate her with his tool. Can you describe this widow so he may locate correctly the one?

She is tiny and coloured and she will not shut up.

My man will fix your window and endeavour so you will satisfied Sir. Will that enough?

That will for a moment. I am finished. God save the Queen.

I hope so.

USEFUL SAYINGS IN THE HOSTEL

Have I received a massage?

That naughty waitress are get the rough edge of my tongue.

At what clock must I evacuate myself?

A CORRESPONDENCE TO THE HOSTEL

Indoors BBQ Club UK (IBCUK)
2 Nevill Gardens
Hove, BN3 7QF

13nd November 2002

The Manager
The Ritz Hotel
150 Piccadilly
London
W1J 9BR

Dear Sir

I became the Secretary to ours indoors barbecue club that is a antitode that the British weathers. We made instead that ours BBQ may be in the indoors environment to avoid raining.

We wish now reserved the room in the Ritz Hotel for a big party with the indoors BBQ. We shall prepared every foods, and the 'guess list' shall include Hove Scotchpipes who play highland tunes and march all over your hotel when guests eat their sausages or your Ritz crackers.

I know you are thinking! Shall this be safe? We made specially the foresight. We will put some wet carpets on the floor and leave ours deadly gas containers in the 'cloaksroom'. The igniting petrol is in a safe plastic tank and we have also the big umbrella on top the cooking flames to stifle the smoke. Do not alarmed that it is unfortunate luck if the umbrella is open indoors – it is the old wife's tail.

Send me some dates at once.

Sincerely yours friend

TOMAS SANTOS

BY APPOINTMENT TO
HRH THE PRINCE OF WALES
SUPPLIERS OF BANQUETING
AND CATERING SERVICES
THE RITZ LONDON

THE RITZ LONDON

London 16th November 2002

Tomas Santos Esq.
2 Nevill Gardens
Hove BN3 7QF

Dear Mr Santos,

Thank you very much for your letter dated 13th November.

Unfortunately we do not allow for indoor BBQ's to be used within the Ritz hotel. As a hotel we cannot take any risks with regards to the safety of our guests and staff.

Thank you for considering the Ritz hotel and please do not hesitate to contact our Food and Beverage department should you require any further information.

Yours sincerely,

Stijn Kuppens
Assistant Food and Beverage Manager

150 PICCADILLY, LONDON W1J 9BR
TELEPHONE (020) 7493 8181   FACSIMILE (020) 7493 2687
ENQUIRE@THERITZLONDON.COM   WWW.THERITZLONDON.COM
CHAIN CODE: LW   TOLL FREE RESERVATIONS FROM THE USA 1 877 748 9536
THE RITZ HOTEL (LONDON) LTD. REGISTERED IN ENGLAND NO 64203C. VAT REGISTRATION NO 420 4790 73

IN THE LIBRARY

The English invented many science, art, law, music, and sophistry. Also the English invented English, to write it all in books. Then they hided them in a library so nobod should know where all the ideas are, or read them. Britain has several public library but this did not made any profits. The dialogue underneath shall improve of your book-learning. No talking.

THE DISCOURSE

Ahoy there everybody! Three cheers to the library.
   Shhhh!
Oh, hello Lady. Your library has the exciting echo.
   May I help you Sir?
Book me.
   Pardon?
I want read a book. I am the book worm.
   Off you go then.
Well, tell what books you have.
   Sir, this the famous British Library. We have quite all the books are published of the English language. What are you looking exactly?
I wish a French book.
   Do you know his name?
Mrs Bovary. It is a anecdote by Gustav Flambée of the lady and

his husband. It is his *magnum opus* of French letters.

You want it of the aboriginal French?

Naturellement.

Anything else?

If you please.

What?

I wish another French book.

Which is…?

Au Revoir Monsieur Pommes Frites. I will translate him in English for exercise.

Sir, If I may say it, I think you should find he is a French interpretating of the English book Goodbye Mr Chips *of James Hilton.*

Do you have: *The Old Pickwick Shop* or *Nicholas Twist?*

And they are by…?

They is recommended reading books of my language school. Both are of Charles Copperfield.

No.

What of *The Nickleby Notes; Sketches by the Hearth; American Cricket; The Curiosity Carol; A Man on the House; Times and Chimes; A Christmas Rudge; The Haunted Son; Barnaby Life; The Battle of Boz; David the Drood; Martin Friend; A Tale of Two Chuzzlewits; Oliver Dombey; Great Cities; Our Mutual Expectations; The Mystery of Edwin Dorrit;* or *Bleak Little Deep Hard Frozen Papers?*

None of it.

Then I should like made just the photostat for my alien visa.

Show me your reproduction equipment and how you like to be turned on?

Sir, I go to the stacks.

Have you the interesting works of Graham Greene: *A Burnt Suit-Case, Our Man In A Van,* or *Travels With My Cunt?*

Goodbye.

Thank for your help, Miss.

USEFUL SAYINGS IN THE LIBRARY

Is this English grammar book an American-English English grammar book or an English-English English grammar book?

Have you *Jamie's Scratch 'n' Sniff TV Cookery Experience?*

Why will the council close you down and sell every books for 50p?

These early colour plates are fantastically valuable. Have you the razor?

Farenheit 451.

Silence.

A CORRESPONDENCE TO
A FAMUOUS AUTHOR

2 Nevill Gardens
Hove, BN3 7QF

2rd May 2001

Henry Fielding
Brigdet Jones' Dairy
Picador
Mc Millan Publishers
25 Eccleston Place
London
SW1W 9NF

Dear Helen

I am visiting in England since a short time to study in the language college. My teacher in English said that I may write a lady – even that I am a unknown boy.

I read yours book: *Bridget Jones' Dairy*. She is the very funny storey that had a merry narration and smiles for hers readerships. Huge Grant is staring in the film and he is the quite movie star. Helen, you can get rich if your movie may be popular, I think yours accountant will tell you the 'farts and figures'.

May I pose to you somes little questions?

- What aminal is you best aminal?
- Do yours hairs or do you the hair piece?
- Do you opinion that beast enlargement is good or that she is evil?

I put the stamp for good responding manners.

Yours friend

Tomas Santos

TOMAS SANTOS

May 23, 2001

Mr.Tomas Santos
2 Nevill Gardens
Hove, East Sussex BN3 7QF

Dear Tomas,

Thank you very much for your letter which made me very happy.

Here are the answers to the questions:

a) Elifant
b) I like peace
c) She is neither good nor evil – just a bit silly

With v.g. wishes,

IN THE PICTURES GALLERY

Many pictures gallery are abundant with painting and decorating. If you like to stare at the nude you could go there. Public exhibitionism is mainly gratuitous in England so why not take advantage of them?

THE DISCOURSE

We are arrived now in the National Pictures Gallery. What shall we view in the first instance?

I don't care less.

Like you the Victorian century?

Yes. Conduct me that I should view the Impersonators.

Follow in this way then. Here are we. These illustritions are indeed fine. What you think them?

I don't like it.

Well, this is *Portrait of the Yellow House* by Van Gogh, and that is his way to painting houses.

Was he insane?

Aye.

And cut his ears off?

Pardon?

I think his front door needs repainting.

What you opinion of this self-portrait by Renoir?

Who's it of?

It is of he.

I like more The Gurning Cavalier.

Oh, fair enough.

This nude is well hung.

Yes indeed. It is by Augustus Leopold Egg.

You like it?

Yes, he was a good egg.

You should be on telly.

Shall we look in the Bacon room? I should like to view more the modern work.

Very well. We must go through sculptures showroom.

What think you here of this notorious woman?

She has a hole in the guts. This statute was craved in the modern way. I will not it. A child could made it!

It is indeed contemporaneous.

It's Monet for old ropes. Let us buy instead some Salvador Dalí mouse mats in the shop and enjoy the cheesecake in the refractory.

Useful sayings of the pictures gallery

I do not know much of art but I know of which I like.

What is it supposed to be?

This one's brilliant, it looks just like a photograph.

I wish to look at Constables and Sergeants.

This video installation is the work of yet another charlatan.

A CORRESPONDENCE TO
THE HOLEY FATHER

Top flat
2 Nevill Gardens
Hove
East Sussex
BN3 7QF
England

20th April 2005

Pope Benedict (XIV)
Papal Apartments
Quite Near St Peter's Basilica
Vatican City

Dear Pope Benedict

I wish congratulate you. It is very much historical to have now the New Pope during a long time years. And you are him.

You were earlier called 'Cardinal Ratzinger, the Enforcer' but now are you 'The Pope' so do not worried if you are not the 'Good Shepherd' but the 'German Shepherd'. Also do not listen the fusspots that you were the Hitler Youth. We all made mistakes. That why there are rubbers on a pencil (not prophylactric contraceptives, of course).

In the news paper I read your history. You have been a dogmatic professor – *Sensible*. You then were the titular Archbishop and Vice Dean of the College of Cardinals. Did you see some phonographic videos?

I hear also you enjoy play piano and smoke 40 a day Marlboro's, like Fat Waller. It must be hard to have a crafty one if you blessing everybody all the time.

Can you send me a singed photo in your funny hat?

God bless, your Holiness.

Yours friend

Tomas Santos

TOMAS SANTOS

PS. Did you knew today was Hitler's brirthday? Will you had a party?

SECRETARIAT OF STATE

FIRST SECTION · GENERAL AFFAIRS

From the Vatican, 8 June 2005

Dear Mr Santos,

The Holy Father has received your letter and he has asked me to thank you. He appreciates the sentiments which prompted you to write to him.

His Holiness will remember you in his prayers and he invokes upon you God's blessings of joy and peace.

Yours sincerely,

Monsignor Gabriele Caccia
Assessor

Mr Tomas Santos
Top flat
2 Neville Gardens
HOVE
East Sussex
BN3 7QF

AT THE GARAGE

In England are rough thoroughfares and ill-metalled byways. Therefore is the vehicle to have a often check-up with the fitter, who will go all over your car for a leak, or otherwise. If you are not tanked up on the highway, AA can give you one for the road. They also shall test your water and blow up your wheels. This realism scenario in the motor garage will cause you to become exercised.

THE DISCOURSE

Good day, Mr Mechanic. My car is ill. I have drived her into the bay.

Has she sinked?

The *parking* bay in your behind.

Yes, I understanded. I merely was joking of you Sir.

Well, do not. I am an alien.

OK, don't bite of my head, mate. What is the trouble your car?

My wife is upset. She drived her merely one week and then she broke down.

Have you been pushing her around?

I dragged her on a rope, after my trailer.

Shall you describe her?

Well, I suppose so: she is a French model.

Tasty. What colour?

She's white.

Is she fast?

Once upon time she had indeed a reputation of it but now is she slowing down. She crawls home after the night out and is horrible screechy. She as well has always a gigantic thirst and can put away gallons. She is costing me the fortune.

How old she?

I shall not say it. Is that consequential?

What about her body?

Pardon?

Describe me her body. I will make a picture in the head.

Well, she was long ago sleek but she is faded and start truly seem her age. She has scratches all over her backside and there is something wrong with her hooter.

Does it make a whistling when she blows it?

You're tell me. Also her spare tyre is unsightly.

Is she starting to smell?

Yes. She gives a foul odour while she climbs the hill to our house. And she smokes heavy as we driving.

From her pipe?

Yes.

Does she dribble?

She do.

I see. How about when she is idle?

She will make a grinding noise when I try to get her going. She used to went like clappers and had an electricity, but her battery seems dried. She has become cold to my touch.

Right. How do you turn her on?

I do it with an old crank. When I put him in the little hole she is always frosty and it takes long before I can turn her over. I put a blanket on her rear end at night and I warm up her in the morning with a hot sponge, and rub on her seat with the oily rag.

What she is like under the covers?

She used to get steamed up easy but now not. Her bottom has a hole in it.

Does she ever have a leak on the floor?

With knobs on! And her boot is jam-packed also of water.

How do you deal it?

I remove her bonnet and clout on her head with a gasket spanner.

Did you think to put her to scraps?

She may old but I still love her. Her bottom has fallen out but she demands only a filling and maybe a screw under the arches.

Does she want one in her bottom?

Worth a try. Can I then drive her away?

Bring her round and push her over my jacking chamber.

I will gather her. You shall hear as I come, for her plates scrape the floors.

Don't fear; I will give her a good servicing.

See you in a small while, then.

Dipstick!

Useful sayings in the garage

My car is broken.
My plugs is chafed.
My nuts have fallen off.
My petrol has run away.
I am unhinged.
Fill me with gas.
My big end is leak.
Oil my change.

The vehicles vocabulary

The gas pedal.
A parking certifcate.
A wheel clam.
The horn.
Carless driving.

AT THE PANTOMIME

In the winter is England a grey land so they invented to a jolly theatrical occasion that called the pantomime to take your mind off its. In the panto will you had the Ugly Sitters, Ali Barber and the 40 burglars, Widow Twankey (is a man in the dress), jolly songs, and the audience precipitation. How sophristicated.

THE DISCOURSE

We have good one seats here on the hippodrome isn't it?

Someone has put sticky on my chair.

Don't be fuzzpot. Did you bought the programme?

I never buy it, they is full adwerts only.

But it has the story inside.

Isn't that the playwright's job?

Yes.

Which time shall curtain up?

Half to 8 clock. Are you excitable? This the story of Peter Pane: the boy who never grown up. He lives in Never Never Land.

Sounds like my granddad.

His friends are lost boys and fairies.

Sounds like my Uncle Vivian.

Other one characters is Captain Hock and Windy and Tinkerbell.

    Why?
I don't knob.
    Can he fly?
With secret wires.
    You spoil everything.
Oh no I don't.
    Oh yes you do.
Oh no I don't!
    Oh yes you don't.
Where's my scarf?
    It's behind you!
Oh no it isn't.
    That's enough. I wish that woman would take of her hat.
Shut up, the light becomes dark and the curtain ascends.
    This always the best bit in the theatre.
Don't forget switch of your moblie phone.
    Pass the Murray Mints.
Shhhh!
    Shhhh yourself!

COMMON ONES PANTOMIME TITLES

Babes in the Hood
Goldilocks and the Beanstalk
Sleeping White
Beauty and the Goose
Dick in Puss

A CORRESPONDENCE TO THE WIZARDS

2 Nevill Gardens
Hove, BN3 7QF

19st October 2002

The Secretary
The Magic Circle
The Centre for the Magic Arts
12 Stephenson Way
London
NW1 2HD

Dear Sir

I went with my landlord daughter in the magic show to the church hall for hers birthday present. We had seen the magic entertainer called Fergal Martin –'The Great Martini. Shaken not stirred.'

Martini start his's cabaret by a amazing trick that hunderds pigeons came out of his pants. But soon his trick begin went wrong and he made extremely swearings such that the vicar wished to terminate him. He said 'P*** Of! I am in the F****** Magic Circle!' and made an old lady cry. A mother came on the stage to prevend him but he wacked on hers nose with his magic rod. He was a greatly smelly man that he had been in the alehouse so I went with some mens on the stage that we should hold him but his assistant lady pours milk on top ours heads from her magic jugs and let his pigeons flew away such that they made 'excreting' everwhere on us.

Then he pushed me such that I fell of the stage and he kicked me in the orchestra stalls. This made my eyes water.

Will you fired The Great Martini from the Magics Circle that is the very known magic society in the world? I hope so, otherwise is the disgraceful.

Yours friend

TOMAS SANTOS

PS: where did his birds came from?

THE
MAGIC CIRCLE

SECRETARY : CHRIS PRATT MIMC
13 CALDER AVENUE BROOKMANS PARK HERTS AL9 7AH
TEL/FAX: 01707 654 971 E-MAIL: prattmsm@hotmail.com

23rd October 2002

Mr. T Santos
2, Nevill Gardens,
Hove,
E. Sussex,
BN3 7QF

Dear Mr. Santos,

Fergal Martin – The Great Martini

Thank you for your recent letter concerning the above-named.

I am sorry to hear of the truly appalling antics of Mr. Martin which must have been very distressing indeed. I have checked through the records of The Magic Circle and I am pleased to say that there is no trace of anyone by the name of Fergal Martin or The Great Martini. If you have any of his promotional material which states to the contrary, perhaps you would let me have sight of it.

If you need a magician in the future, please do not hesitate to contact me.

Yours sincerely,

CHRIS PRATT
SECRETARY

TO THE PUB

The pub is the British tradition and unique. Much beer is warm or without bubbles so drink of wine. Always introduce yourself into a woman and give her man the clap on his back. Tell to him: 'Sir, I am enamoured of your girl; how old is it?' Or, 'Hello my old Chinese, are you rich?' Cheers.

THE DISCOURSE

Good day bar man. I should take two litres ale.

Very well, Sir.

How much guineas will that cost mate?

Wait. I compute him. It shall little money – merely £2.

Thank to you my ogod man. I now shall speaking this pretty lady. Good night you pretty lady. May I seat me or have you reservations?

Not at all, Sir. Sit on my right hand. Come you another land by chance?

Yes, you detected me. I am exotic.

You speak well English even.

I learn it with the book. She named itself *Found in Translation* and I am fluid.

I don't blamed you.

Shall you some eatings morsel or a drinks Miss?

No thank.

Allow me to press you.

Then I give up. I wish a goblet Scottish on the stones and the packet salty and onion potato chips.

Wait in a moment and I come again with mouthfuls. I will buy also one packet smokings.

Oh not! It should canker my bronichals.

Then drink well.

And with you comrade.

Useful sayings in the pub

Mine's a large one.

Cheerio to your good health.

Up your bottoms.

Are you coming down the Cock?

No smoke.

At what clock are your pubes open in England?

Time gentlemens please.

Cussing Vocabulary

Oh bother!

Oh lawks!

Oh rot!

Oh mercy!

Oh Chris!

Suck me fideways!

A CORRESPONDENCE TO DEIDRE AGONY

Top flat
2 Nevill Gardens
Hove, BN3 7QF

15st November 2002

Deidre Sanders, *The Sun* Agony Aunt
The Sun
Problem Page
1 Virgina Street
London
E98 1AX

Dear Deidre Aunt

The other day I must went in my land lord's attic to search some values I put in there. I got the hook pole to opened the hatch but he sprang opened and showers dead one insects and spiders fell on me. I leapt sideway but I hit onto the table that my cup tea was on it and he fell on my toes and smashed, and the scorching liquids absorped in my sock. So I drew off my sock to blow on my smarting foot but I trod onto the sharp cup splinters's with torment and I cursed (God save me).

I pulled then the steps from the 'hatch' with my pole but the small bit metal fell off and the steps unrolled with alacricity and bashed on my head with the clang noise and my spectacle fell off. I travelled up the attic steps in a wobbly mode to switched the lighting button but no light came. I elongatered my arms to put the pole in the hatch, such that I should go up to put the fuses, but it hit on a tin of nails that now bashed on my head with torture and I heavily fell down the steps to the ground. What a shame that the floors had sharp nails. I had not my glasses and I was bit blind and I trod hard on the unvisible nails with my nudely feets. I jumped away and treaded then on my spectacles and broke it with a snapping. This was the 'last straw hat broke the camel's back' so I gave up it and put the hook inside a loop to push upwards the steps. But they ladders went in to fast and disappeared, and dust sprinkled in the sun shine. I pulled away the pole but was it lodged. So I made the strong pull and at once the hook came off and I was running fast backward along the landing strip and clung the pole for 'dead life'. In a moment I met the stairs and tumbled completely to the bottom and broke my legs and the stick went in my eye.

I am bit fed up, what can you suggested?

Yours friend

TOMAS SANTOS

NEWS GROUP NEWSPAPERS LTD

From: Deidre Sanders, Problem Page Editor, 1 Virginia Street London E98 1AX Telephone: 020 7782 4000.

3rd December 2002.

Tomas Santos,
Top Flat,
2 Nevill Gardens,
Hove BN3 7QF.

Dear Tomas,

I'm not surprised you are stressed with a series of events as you have described in your letter.

I hope things will quieten down for you and life will become straightforward for you once again very soon. Meanwhile, my leaflet on stress is enclosed for you.

With best wishes,

Yours sincerely,

Deidre Sanders.

Registered Office, News Group Newspapers Ltd., 1 Virginia Street, London E98 1XY.
Registered No. 679215 England

AT THE VILLAGE CRICKET GAME

The cricket is a sport for Englishmen with very hard balls. It is mysterious for the visitor that English get fun to see 11 men play with themselves in their white trousers. These discourse will assist to made you understand to the ancient sport.

THE DISCOURSE

Good afternoon Vicar. It is warmly in the pavilion. Will you explicate me the laws of the cricket for I am foxed?

With pleasure, my old fruit. This is the game that my four fathers. It is easy as falling of a log. You must first two sides. One side is outside on the cricket court and one side shall linger inside the pavilion. One man that is in the side that is inside must go and be in outside but when he is out he must come in and the another inside man will go out and be in until he is out. When all the outside side are out they shall come in and those that are the inside side must go out and get the outside side that now go in out.

That is clear. But who is this running fellow?

That is Mr Nichols. He is a tosser.

I could agree more.

You observe his balls? They are nine inches of circumference and he may rub them on his trouser or also put spittles on them to be brilliant. In sometimes may he polish 'nose greases' on them so they shall wobble in the air.

Will he then throw him?

He must not throw, he must 'bowl' it. You see he must not jerk under his arm or he will be called 'no balls'. If he will cause the Leg Before Wicket (BMW) the other shall be out and go in.

May a woman play it?

Indeed, Sir. I teach the ladies a lesson. On Friday night I showed them my yorker in the Scout hut.

Did you score, Vicar?

No. They fight like tigers. Mrs Banting handles my googlies with no troubles and Mrs Best also can take a full toss in her sleep. But she is the sporty woman. You know she makes sport massages to the farmers' rowing club?

Yes, Vicar. I have seen her in the gym, rubbing down their cox.

Careful, you nearly knocked my pint over.

Tell me, Vicar, why does the doctor arrive always in his hospitals coat.

He is not doctor, you silly, he is the Empire. He will watch and gesticulate his judgments to the scorings board with movements.

Then who is this fellow with gauntlets?

He is the wicked keeper. You observe also the captain has a Short Leg and a Silly behind?

Yes, he has his hand down his pants.

You charlie. He only adjusts his box.

So, when all his men are gone the races each are counted?

Exactly.

How exciting.

Oh I say! Mr Nichols is out for a duckling.

Vicar, please explain me what is 'The Ashes'.

Burnt sticks in a tin. But forgive me, I must put my armour to be the next beater to go in the field.

What is 'the follow-on'?

Excuse me, I want to play badly.

What is a 'dead ball'?

I must go.

What means 'One short'?

Good afternoon!

I hope you will score the goal Vicar.

You are a fruitcake, Sir.

USEFUL SAYINGS OF CRICKET

Who is wining?

Did we again lose?

Owzat!

Oh bother! Bad light stopped play.

AT THE SEA SIDE

The sea sides of UK is frolicsome and the English are laughable. Smile at the native who paddled with the trouser up and the neckerchief on his pate. Put a penny to see what the butter saw or eat of gelatine cones, of burghers, and of the infamous English luncheon: fishes and crisps. But put always the sun shield to avoid skin canker.

THE DISCOURSE

Hello, Mr Tourist Officer. What time do Lancashire open?

We never close.

Will you welcome me then in your town?

Indeed Sir: this is my town and you are welcome to it.

Why are you so attractive?

Well, we have extremely facilities for the families and the delicious beach for bathe or for sunning, and all is secure. We have handsome live guards and you safely may dip the waters in your swim pants.

Then I shall put on my 'budgie smugglers' and my sister will made a bikini test in the brine.

Captain Trelawney makes the boat expedition for the fishings. Should she delight in that?

Will she catch crabs?

Our harbour must enjoy well currents for the crabs to aggregate.

Do you have a sandy bottom?

We have of gravel and of sandy both. Attend me and I shall show you it is clean.

Super.

Here, look at my front. See the spectacle. We have the sands; the aquatic memorial; the piddling pool of childrens; manifold feeding kiosks; the candy froth emporium, and confections.

Tasty.

Of our sea shore we have the jackass ride, the bathings, the toilets, and the keck chairs. The swells rush on the beach and many bath in the safe waters.

I find that hard to swallow, what with this crud oil on every side.

Look; see there. The ladies do play volleyball in their bikini. They husbands also is leaping and are catch his balls in a jaunty disposition.

Oh I say, Miss, what a terrific snatch! I like increasingly your town, Mate. She is a bonny environs.

Indeed, the seas are waving, the sun belts down and the peoples are having ecstasy in the water.

But what is leaking of that brown pipe?

It is of no interesting.

Is it ordure?

Let us quick go on the neighbourhood and you shall see such that we experience ever sun shine in ours municipality.

But do you have some of amusements here?

Why yes. Look of the esplanade; we have multifarious they.

I want to go in your ghost train and look at your ghoulies in the dark.

You shall scream of terror at the hairy monsters. Will you not prefer to come in the bummer cars?

No. I should sick me. Can you are suggest some others pass time?

Take a hike.

I have an ill leg for climbing. I would more like golf.

Be my guset. I can look after your ball bag.

Ah. Unhappily, am I complete rusted of the game and I am badly handicapped.

This is hard work.

What will you do of your holiday, Mr Tourist Officer?

I am going to Masbate for sixteen days.

I beggar your pardon?

It is a sunny aisle of the Philippines.

The Canaries were the last resort for me.

Are you the ornithologist?

No. Notwithstanding, I must fly.

OK then.

Cheers mate.

Keep it real bro.

USEFUL SAYINGS OF THE SEA SIDE

Kiss my quick.

Cream my nose.

Who leaves all these beer tins?

Sand is everywhere in my foods.

My ice cream has dissolved.

Have you got the Diocalm?

HOLIDAYS VOCABULARY

Airplane.

The slimming pool.

Germans.

Towels.

Decks chair.

Calamari.

The reprisal Montezuma.

The photos.

A sand palace.

Skin burn.

A CORRESPONDENCE TO A AIRFIELD

Top flat
2 Nevill Gardens
Hove, BN3 7QF

11st October 2002

The Director
Parham Airfield
Pulborough Road
Cootham
Pulborough
RH20 4HP

Dear Sir

I would to join yours gilding club that I may fly the gliders to made relaxing. It is the pieceful time in the skys to forgot your trouble. I am with extremely the enthusiasm so please tell me the joining arrangement that I shall arrive immediately. I put the stamp for courtesy.

Another club I was before will not allow me again because I forgot my narcolepsy pill such that I went a bit asleep. But it was fortuanately we were not yet in the sky so I only smashed one wing slightly and one the wheels fell off. I think my guardian angle was looked after me.

'See you soon'.

Your sincerely

TOMAS SANTOS

TOMAS SANTOS

PS: excuse that my hand writings is bit bent. I hurted my arms in a car crash.

Southdown Gliding Club

website: www.southdown-gc.demon.co.uk

T.Santos
Top Flat
2 Nevill Gardens
Hove
BN3 7QF

Telephone: 01903 742137
01903 746706   Members Line
E.Mail: southdown@sephton30.freeserve.co.uk

Date   20.10.2002

Dear Mr Santos,

With regard to your letter dated 11th October 2002 requesting joining information for the Southdown Gliding Club.

As you will no doubt appreciate the most important aspect of all forms of aviation is that of Safety both for the participants and for all other members of the public.

I have discussed your situation with both the Club Chairman and the Chief Flying Instructor and they have advised me that with your Medical condition we are unable to invite you to become a Member of this club.

It is with regret that we have come to this decision and we hope that you will find satisfaction elsewhere.

Yours sincerely

J.L Cook
Membership Secretary.

The Southdown Gliding Club Limited
Member of the British Gliding Association

Registered in England No 11531R

Registered Office: Parham Airfield, Pulborough Road, Cootham
Pulborough, West Sussex RH20 4HP

IN THE TEA SHOP AND CAFÉ

The British had an elaborate ceremony to tea time such that cream-tea and sconce with battered toasts. In the café do not sit at once, for firstly must you shake everybody over his coffee. It is done in UK. In the 'Olde English Tea Shoppe' the man ever grasps his lumps with a sugars tong. Afterwards they wash the tea pot and stand upside-down on the drain boards.

THE DISCOURSE

Miss, we are ready to our tea.

Yes, Sir. What you want you?

Percolade me two cups tea if you will.

Typhoid or Earl Grey?

What is he?

He is a delicious, infused with oils of aromatic bergamot.

Normal.

And for food?

I am ravishing and I could eat a house.

Do you fancy some of gateau perhaps?

May I get crumpet here?

With pleasure, Sir.

Give me six of the best.

Shall I spread them for you, or would you desire some else also?

Well, I was admiring your fantastic baps.

Thank you.

Will you show me your muffins also?

Take a look at these! Are you satisfied?

I love it. But Miss, I cannot removed the hood of my jam pot.

Sir, are you go round the twist?

I have done the twist two times but he will not become unattached. How then?

Push off.

Eureka! It has fallen.

Your teapot arrives, Sir. May I milk you?

Your jugs are large Mrs.

One lump or two?

I will cream myself.

You don't say.

Can you recommend the best tart in your establishment?

Do you want a spotted dick?

Sauce.

USEFUL SAYINGS IN THE TEA SHOP

Nice buns, lady.

I take a besprinkled fritter.

Give me a tongue sandwich Madam.

Your self-service is courteous.

Is this tea or just hot water with smell of fruits?

Get your laughing gear round that, girl.

A CORRESPONDENCE TO THE SPICIERS

2 Nevill Gardens
Hove, BN3 7QF

3st October 2002

Enquiry department
Lea £ Perrins Ltd
Worcetser
Sauce
WR5 1DT

Dear Customer Enquiry

I had visiting in UK since the quite short time to 'make myself at home'. One the exciting substance such that I had discovered him is 'The Original & Genuine Lea & Perrins Worcestershire sauce' by 'Royal appointment' with the Queen of England. Excellent! It has the typical flavor of England ('Adds instant richness!').

I send many bottle to my mother oversea to made the soups and the recipes but I have a questions of the ingredients:

Malt vinegar
Spirt vinegar
Molasses
Sugar
Salts
Anchovies (golly)
Tamarins (!)
Onoins
Garlics
Specis
Flavoring

Why is there is tamarins in it? Did you put in his tails? How do you catch such marmosets? Will it damage my kidney if I shall eat to much? I anticipate yours response with some a bit nervous.

Yours friend

TOMAS SANTOS

PS I hope the Royal Queen didn't got a belly ache from it.

HP Foods Limited

Please reply to :-
HP Foods Limited, Tower Road, Aston Cross, Birmingham, B6 5AB
Tel : 0121 - 359 4911 : Fax : 0121 - 380 2335

Our Ref: 4766

11 October 2002

Mr Santos
2 Mevill Gardens
Hove
Brighton
BN3 7QF

Dear Mr Santos

Re: Lea & Perrins Worcestershire Sauce

Thank you for your recent letter and your compliments on our sauce. We are extremely pleased that you and your family enjoy it so much.

The ingredients are as you have written but some of your spelling is incorrect:

Malt Vinegar, Spirit Vinegar, Molasses, Sugar, Salt, Anchovies, tamarinds, onions, garlic, spices and flavouring

The anchovies are a type of fish and tamarinds are a tropical fruit (not tamarins which are monkeys!)

There is no reason why our sauce should damage your kidneys unless you are eating very large amounts of it.

We enclose a product voucher towards your next purchase and hope you continue to enjoy our products.

Thank you again and good luck with your English studies.

Yours sincerely

roduct Voucher

A DANONE GROUP COMPANY

IN THE WORK OFFICE

If you are an alien you could made work in UK only with a lawful paper. You can did nice job to wash a sink in the pubic house, or if you speak well English you may traduce language in a office. Here some dialogue of the work office to familiar you.

THE DISCOURSE

Good Morning, Tracy. How was the week end go?

Oh Sharon, I am browned of. I have the dumps. I have lachrymose. I am misery.

Well, I mean that is quite a bit surprise. Say it what the matter. The problem shared is the problem divided.

I am fool. I should listened of your warns, for Colin has unloaded of me. I am abandoned of my suitor.

I said you that he was an cad and the bounder. Is he attached to another, Tracy?

I cannot speak of it or I should weep me.

Place your head on my soldier.

No. I shall master my sentiments and he can just feck of himself!

Do not cuss Tracy. It is ill of a lady. I know what ails you. You need something hot inside you. Let us got coffees out of the machinery.

Very well. What gossips or hearsay know you, Sharon, to take my memory away my problems?

Did you heard, Jameela said Wendy in Finance has the newly girl baby?

What is her name is?

Jameela.

No.

Wendy.

No, the suckling tot.

Chardonnay Kylie Beckham Smith. Here's your coffee.

Oh, that is fair nomenclature. What the hell is this?

Well, I pushed of the coffee indicator but nevertheless came this green soup.

You know, Sharon, mens are similar all them. Ale and curry and the foot ball merely are his pleasure. Never he understands to romance of a lady with candles, cosy dinner or Barry Manilow. He wishes only to rental of the salacious DVD and make the belch contest with his familiars.

Tell me about it. Crumbs! It is half past to eleven and I should already inspect of Charles's inbox and prepare for his dictations or shall I be in bad odour.

Oh Sharon, you have the best one boss. He is pretty. He is puissant. He has a resplendent eye and he faints every woman for he looks exactly as Bertrand Russell.

Do you mean Russell Crowe?

That's it. Oh God's blood! He comes now and my facial eye-woad requires of a touch up. I will run away. See you for the lunchbox in an half hour.

Yea, I could do with a stiff one.

Good morning Sharon. Where has young Tracy disappear so alacrity?

She is a busy today Charles. Are you well adjusted to dictate to me?

Of which?

The letters.

Go in my office and I will come in a jiffy.

OK.

You are a super, Sharon. You are a fast lady and also you do me well with your short hand, and you keep abreast on my diary.

Charles, I just am a working girl.

Right, I dictate of the letter. Are you poised?

Yea.

This it: Dear Sir, I answer to your suggest that we are incompetent of our business. You must know that we are an innovative and client-focused inside-out enabler organization facilitating sticky web-readiness with transforming bespoke turnkey options for growth-centred enterprise brands. Utilizing best practice no-blame strategics and quality-driven benchmark channel implementation, our engineered viral e-services drivers and tailored dot-com action items parent key push-pull strategies off-line to monetize your company's hardball message paradigms going forward. We focus on big-picture base covering and our thinking-outside-the-box and gap-analysis imperatives check below-the-line free-fall and flag best-of-breed incubators at brainstorm stage. Our top-down upscaled magic bullet solutioning means added client value in incentivizing core business feedback input from goal-directed B2B e-tailer throughput optimizing, delivering low-ceiling win-win value-added outputs with cut-to-fit synergistic firewall-friendly SME bandwidthing initiatives, providing showstopper turnarounds and actioning innovative partner-facing growth-based bottom-up scaleable solutions. Building on our track record of iterative short haul re-envisioneered synergies, and seamless service interoperability, our repurposeable leading-edge thoughtware streaming delivers results-driven tactical future-proof asset value, seamlessly empowering your mission-critical image-enterprise thought-leadership with leverageable global knowledge-management and proactive outcome-centred eyeballing deliverables. So, I cast-off your unmannerly allegations, Sir, and dismiss you as a vexatious alligator. Yours etc…. Got that?

I shall type up it for you.

Get on with it then.

USEFUL SAYINGS FOR THE WORK OFFICE

Sign this leaving card.

These appraisals are just crap, aren't they?

I've only went five minutes and I have me 66 new e-mails.

That Stuart has so far up the boss's fundament his merely feet are stick out.

Downsizing.

Redundance.

P45.

A CORRESPONDENCE TO AN JOURNAL

'Go Away!'
2 Nevill Gardens
Hove, BN3 7QF

14rd October 2002

Commissioning Editor
Travel Desk
The Guradain
119 Farringdon Road
London
EC1R 3ER

Dear Sir

I wonder you will write the 'story' of my exciting new business idea in the travels section of *The Gurdian*, with a interview of me and the smiling photograph.

My business idea is for the travel company. This will called Go Away! and the Unique Selling Proposition (IUD) is such that if customers come to us we will just send them away. We will tell them where to go and where to get off.

So, I shall visit in yours office next Friday to discus the story with a cup tea.

Yours friend

[signature]

TOMAS SANTOS
Go Away!

119 Farringdon Road, London EC1R 3ER
Telephone 020 7278 2332
guardian.co.uk

Tomas Santos
Go Away!
2 Nevill Gardens
Hove
BN3 7QF

18ᵗʰ December 2002

Dear Tomas Santos

Thank you for your letter suggesting a feature based on your travel company. We read your proposal with interest but we are unable to pursue the idea. We didn't think the piece would work for us, but we wish you all the best with approaching other publications with your suggestion.

Thank you for thinking of the Guardian.

Yours sincerely

Clare Brown
Administrator

Guardian Travel Desk

Guardian Newspapers Limited
A member of Guardian Media Group PLC
Registered Office
164 Deansgate, Manchester M60 2RR
Telephone 0161 832 7200
Registered in England Number 908396

A CORRESPONDENCE TO A LLAMA

Top Flat
2 Nevill Gardens
Hove, East Sussex
BN3 7QF

6nd July 2005

His Holiness the Dalai Llama
C/o Tibbetian Government-in-Exile
Dharamsala
Northern India
Asia
World

Dear Dalai

Today is yours 70st birthday. I wish therefore say: *Happy birthday to you, Happy birthday to you, Happy birthday dear Dalai, Happy birthday to yooooouuu!*

You live the life that a simple monk: e.g, no smoking, no drunking, and no especially womans. But only to made the yoga and the transcendental mediation. Sounds possibly a bit boring. What about the entertainments? For example, what are you will do in your birthday party? Do you eat of the cake or will you rather fancy to eat the chips? Then would you be the chip monk.

Can you send me the singed photo with your maroon sheet on? (Look inscrutable, please.)

I put the stamps that you may not spend moneys for good responding manners.

Thanks Holiness.

Keep spiritual.

Yours friend

Tomas Santos

TOMAS SANTOS

PS. Why are you bald?

Tomas Santos
Top Flat 2 Nevill
Hove, East Susse
BN3 7QF
U.K.

OFFICE OF THE H.H. THE DALAI LA
Mcleod Ganj - 176219
DHARAMSALA
Distt. Kangra (H.P.) India

VISITING IN THE ZOO

In England are many zoo. This word is abbreviation for the zoological gradens. A zoo have many animales in a cage, such that a wasp, or in the bath of water, such that a peguin. Here are an exploring dialogue to help you went in the zoo.

THE DISCOURSE

Here we are in the zoo arrived. What animal shall we view it?

I want a ice cream.

Let us see first the monkeys, over here.

Look, he is play a game with the another monkey.

Oh look at they, so like a humang bein. It makes me to laugh me.

Why he climbed on hers back and made moving?

It is perhaps they play the monkey hopscotch.

He is jump too low.

Let us go away now.

Oh look, here is the lions.

The man lion have the luxurous mane. What is he eat?

It looks as a horse.

Oh horrors! Let us go see the Snowdon cage. It is a famous wire building.

Oh yes, see the owl, the condor, and the bird of pray?

No. He is all sleeping. Let us instead to the dark house to

look at the loris, the lemur, the bus baby, and the tarsia with huge eyes.

It is very dark black in here.

Ouch! You careless, you trod my corn.

You have too much big feet.

I see no animals here. It is a waste. What about the peguin, let us go out and see him.

Oh yes, outside is more light. See, look now, the peguin are eat my sandwich. He likes Bovril.

Oi! You two clowns. It says 'Don't food the peguins'!

Oh dear, I am a naughty.

Quick, let us go in the spider house.

I don't not like the creepy arachnoids.

In here then, past these plastic curtain doors, to see the bats.

Oh no! I cannot breath me. It is a odour of pneumonia.

Ammonia.

I don't care. I want go home.

Well, that was fun.

No.

USEFUL SAYINGS IN THE ZOO

Grizzled bear.

Loins and tiggers.

Don't climb over that fence!

Perodicticus potto edwardsi.

ANIMALS VOCABULARY

The cat.
The doges.
A hare.
A seeds.
A wolfs.
An horse.
A Leo.
Orang.

A CORRESPONDENCE TO THE PRIMATES

2 Nevill Gardens
Hove, BN3 7QF

6st March 2002

The Most Reverend Robert Eames LLB, Ph. D Lord Archbishop of Armagh and
Primate of all Ireland
The See Horse
Cathedral Close
Armagh
BT61 7EE

Dear Primate

I greet you with my feelings. I have in UK since two months to made the English
study in my language school that I now correspond you to know a answer that
made me 'scratch the head'.

I enquired to the dictionary to discover that 'Primate' is a ape monkey. Shall
some body is 'pulling my legs'? Will your to forgive my bad letter to explain me
what it, for I wish speak the organ grinder, not the monkey.

As well to that, there is another Archbishop Primate to Ireland. He is 'The Most
Rev. Dr. Sean Brady DCL, Primate of all Iceland'. Why is it two primates? Are
one of you the marmoset and another is the gorilla? In any cases, please put my
wishes to the other one Primate Rev. Dr Brady so I should save my stamps.

God bless you Robert.

Don't eat to many bananas!

Yours friend

TOMAS SANTOS

Archbishop of Armagh

The Most Reverend Dr. R. H. A. Eames

The See House, Cathedral Close, Armagh BT61 7EE Northern Ireland
Telephone: Home (028) 3752 2851   **Office:** (028) 3752 7144   **Fax:** (028) 3752 7823
Email: <archbishop@armagh.anglican.org>

7 March 2002

Mr Tomas Santos
2 Nevill Gardens
Hove BN3 7QF
England.

Dear Mr Santos,

The Archbishop has asked me to thank you for your recent letter.

The term 'Primate' denotes the senior Archbishop in Ireland in both the Anglican and Roman Catholic traditions.   It is an ecclesiastical term and applies to both Archbishops of Armagh for historical reasons.

Yours sincerely,

(Mrs) Roberta Harvey
Archbishop's Secretary.

VISITING IN THE SANATORIUM

All English asylum and hospital have a pretty nurse under a sister under a fat matron under a doctor under a sturgeon under a professor. The hospital is the home to thermometers, bed bathing, throat gurgles, drugs, syringes, morphine, and tragic medical accidents. This dialogue has the vocabularies for you to speak when you visit a unhealthy person in the sanatorium hospital.

THE DISCOURSE

Hello nurse. Gee Whillikins, it is very much hot coming up those stairs of your. Do not you find it is too much warm in here?

Yes, Sir.

You could force cucumbers in your downstairs passage.

Well, we must warm our sick.

Yes, you do not want cold sick.

No.

Look, I am to visit my friend Mr Fleming in Mengele ward. He had his appendices off. Will you show me into his bed?

The client you wish visit is yet on the trolley. There, by the laundry shoot.

Thank.

A pleasure.

Hello there Flem. That nurse have well legs, isn't it?

I suppose. Welcome to my bed, friend. I am pleased of the

companion for I became wearied of nothing. Sit you and let us have some quiet intercourse.

This will cheer you. I have bring for you gifts: of pickle eggs, of piglet's tongue, of brown ale, and some cigars.

Conceal it at once. Dr Phibes forbade me smoke. My vessels are not shipshape as they are ruined of smoking. They make ever tests and today I must have the blood count.

Darcula?

Oh don't not cause me laugh. It makes pull my sewings and it suffers.

I know. When I went in the hospital it was discovered sugar and albumin in my specimen urines.

Oh dear. Can you make children?

No, but I produce well meringues.

You are pull my legs once more.

Yes. Do they care well you in here, mate? Is it the world-class hospital?

I would recommend others. Their pharmacy has dispensed with accuracy, and their behaviour leaves me nothing to hope for.

 Excellent. How are your food?

Today I may choose Blood Sausages in a Rich Grave, Intestines Surprise, or the 'healthy option': Nuts Baked Hard on Yeast and Heated Prunes. So I suffer always the green-apple quickstep.

Inconvenient.

Yes, I'm up and down like a bride's nightie.

You know, hospitals are smell funny. They give me fear. I had to drinked a couple beer in The Fox to give me of intestinal fartitude.

Will you pass the fizzy water?

Pardon?

I must now take my capulets. It is the hour. Please pass the bottle.

Oh I see. Here is your beverage. How else may I do?

Pass me that emesis basin.

Will you be vomit?

No, I need put all these pills somewhere.

Hey, look, I can spring your bed up or down such that you are bounced.

I think appointment hour is finished, if you don't not mind. I am flagging.

Yes, you look real ill.

Thank you.

Get well soon friend and come for a home improvement to be right as ninepence.

Farewell.

Yes, fartwell.

USEFUL SAYINGS IN THE SANATORIA

Blood gases.
Crash trolley.
MRSA.
Necrotizing fasciitis.
Bowl movement.

A CORRESPONDENCE TO THE HOSPITALS PRIEST

2 Nevill Gardens
Hove, BN3 7QF

4st October 2002

The Chaplain
The Royal Sussex County Hospital
Eastern Road
Brighton
BN2 5BE

Dear Reverend

I am visiting in England to study to the English language and develop in UK the music of my home land. Therefore the Scotch pipe is the new insturment for me so I have joined in the new pipes band. My band requires now to rent yours chapel to made some practisings that we may play *Scotchland the Brave, Cock Up Your Beaver* (Robert Bums), *Fanny Power* (W. B. Yeast), *Donald Where's Yer Troosers* (Any Stewart), and much others highland snogs.

We need your chapel every Sunday 9am until 12.30pm. Usually it always goes completely wrong but do not alarmed that we always make a few beginning noises such that very loud screaming and some quite many extremely long screechings (by mistakes). We obey the heath & safety orders and always made sure all windows should to be open.

We shall come out the practising room a bit that we may march in ours Scotch uniforms with tartan kilts (is the type of a man-skirt) and we have knifes in ours socks. We shall then march about the buildings and play a bit loudly but all our moblie phone shall be only in a 'vibrating' mood inside the sporran so your sick shall be undisturbed of ringing.

We shall come next Saturday with the pipes. Write me at once to give me the rentings detail. I put the stamp for courtesy.

Yours friend

TOMAS SANTOS

Chaplaincy
Spiritual Care

Brighton and Sussex **NHS**
University Hospitals
NHS Trust

Chaplaincy Department
The Royal Sussex County Hospital
Eastern Road
Brighton
BN2 5BE

Tomas Santos
Hove Scotchpipes
2 Nevill Gardens
Hove
BN3 7QF

9 October, 2002

Dear Tomas Santos:

HOVE SCOTCHPIPES

Thank you for your letter of 4 October, 2002.

I very much regret that it will not be possible for your group to use the Hospital Chapel to practise the bagpipes.

The Chapel is used every Sunday morning for a service of Christian worship.

And at other times, the Chapel has to be available for patients, relatives and members of staff to use it as a place of peace and quiet.

It would be quite impossible for you to march around the building playing the bagpipes. This could disturb the patients on the wards who are critically ill.

I am sorry we cannot help you with this.   Have you thought of approaching local churches to see if you could use a room in their church hall?

With every good wish.

Yours sincerely,

Richard Adfield (Revd)
Senior Chaplain

AT THE LAUNDRY

To clean your clothes in England why not visit in the launderette? You can done it youself with the machine or if you paid a lady she can scrub you pants and cleanse you of your filth. Why not leave your clothing with her and spend the day having a good time?

THE DISCOURSE

Hello lady I wish wash my smalls.

You wish wash your smalls?

I wish wash my smalls.

Go on then.

How may I done it?

Put him first in the tub and make then some soap flake in your hole.

Will he be cleansed?

Are you ninny? You must push first on the iron nipple to made rotating.

How it?

Oh gawd! Here, let me help you. Put yours garmends in this basket and transfer him inside the vacant tub.

I have made them in the basket. I immediately shall put him in the porthole.

But your whites are mixed with the colour-tainted cloths. You should stain to your dresses or had pink pants.

Shall I cast my smalls to the ground for made a separation?

Look, you do the whites and I'll put these colours in the vacant drum for you.

Lady!

What?

I have put my white ones now in the drum.

Made then the soap! Can you do nothing for yourself?

I have not soap.

Try the dispenser on the wall.

I have not coin, merely a tenner pounds note bill.

Change machine!

OK, I have now the moneys and all is prepared in my white washings. How your colourful load?

It is ready. Give me some your change so we can made these washers circulate.

Will waters come and rinse it?

As soon you press the buttons.

How shall it dried?

You spin it, and then it went in the dry machine.

Lady!

What?

I have forgot this sock.

Urgh! You should chuck it away, it's got a huge hole in the toe.

Pardon?

Oh, do it in the sink if you're that bothered.

Lady!

What?

Thank you to help me schlep my wetwash in the Laundromat.

You haven't got a clue, have you?

USEFUL SAYINGS IN THE LAUNDRY

I drop my knickers until tonight.
I have defiled my breeches.
Please take my clothes off me.
My costume is shrinken.

TO MEET THE QUEEN

In English society or Welch and Scotch or North[ern] Ireland is many way you must to speak to a important VIP (Very Impotant People). This how to have good manners, correctly to tug the fetlock, and address the noble royalties or the upper crust. We begin with to meet the Queen.

THE DISCOURSE

Hello Queen.

Hello man. Why you are hanging around in the ball room?

It's these hired trousers. Can you see it from there?

Did you enjoyed the military band?

Yes, their marital music has a prehistoric rhythm.

They musicians is of the Royal African Rifles.

I do not wish controvert you, Queen, but I think they isn't. They are but English paleface men's.

Well, you are looking at their officers: only their privates are black.

Swipe me!

Funny, isn't it?

Funny pecular, you mean. I see your guests includes tonight also sundry actors.

You're not one of those, are you?

One of those what? I am visiting in England from my home land.

Are you with the Consulate?

No.

Would you drink of wine or dine some Twiglets? My liveried mens have it.

Did you cook it?

Don't be stupid. My servant did it.

No thanks, Your Majestic. I had a kebab at the bus stop and I am a bit full up.

Have you been here long?

Yes.

Are you learn English?

Very much. This is a nice palace you've got here.

Yes.

She is beautiful as the hanging baskets of Babylon

Where you live you?

South England. How about yourself?

I live in these palaces.

They are so much grand. And this masquerade of Prince Philip is the resplendent occasion. It is completely enormous.

Ah yes, the Duke of Edinburgh's balls are the largest in Europe.

And all are dressed so fancy. You look ambrosial in your refinery, Queen. Your diadem sparkles.

But you should see the Price of Wales. His family jewels are the big ones.

Say, Your Majestic, where is your dogs?

We shut him in the pup house.

My landlady's pussy has three legs.

Cripes!

A ambulance squashed on it so it now is bald and can drink only soup.

Well, it's been so interesting to learn all about you. Please excuse me.

I know what you mean. I must strain my potatoes also. Where's your karsy?

Speak at the yonder footman and he will take you up the back stairs.

Oh, you are awful. That is a funny joke Elizabeth. I spilt my sides.

Well, anyway. Until we again should meet.

Yes, see you round, Queen. *Vivat Regina!*

USEFUL MODES TO ADDRESS VIPs

The king: Your Majestic

The queen: Your Majestic

The knight: Good Knight

The viscount: Good Lord

The arch bishop: Good Gracious

The judge: Your Lud

The earl: Earl Hines

The duke: Duke Ellington

The count: Count Basie

The baronet: Hello

A CORRESPONDENCE TO A QUEEN

2 Nevill Gardens
Hove, BN3 7QF

1rd March 2002

Queen Elizabeth (II)
Buckingham Palace
Near Victoria Station
London

Dear Queen Elizabeth

I'm am visting in UK since three months to learn the English. I speak now well that my teacher had encouraged I shall drop you the line.

I am looking forwards yours Golden Jubbly. It shall be remarkably fantastic and you will made a party in Buckingham Place. So I ask now a request: can I visit to your party? Do not alarmed that I should be tatty; I shall dress in my refinery and put my most civilised costume. Please send the invitations card (and the map) at once. I put a stamp for you. Shall I bring some tins beer or will you to prefer something more stronger? Make sure you get some nice snacks and spicey dips.

Shall Price Phillip come in the party? I cannot try to keep up his drinkings, such that he can drink as the fish but I look forwards to see Prince Charles and Camilla Parka Bowels.

I put now some enquiry:

* Is Prince Anne a bit bossy?
* What is your favourite crown?
* Are you tired of waving?

Vivat Regina!

Yours friend

TOMAS SANTOS

PS. If the party is a bit late can I crash on your floor?

2 Nevill Gardens
Hove, BN3 7QF

1th November 2002

Her Majesty the Queen
Buckingham Palace
The Mall
(Green Park End)
London

Dear Queen

I sent you before the letter with some the questions. But I had not the response and I went suddenly in my home land that my mother become unwell that she contracted the malady from a fruit.

I put the stamp into the previous correspondence such that you should conserve the postage, but now is it severeal moths and nothing came.

It perhaps could be such that the letter was mislaid that you have busy office or in the postal service. So I put *again* the stamp such that you may respond. I should wish very much you may sent the singed photo your majesty but if it impossible maybe you should please return my stamps? They are quite expensive. (Or you could sign on the stamp, because it is already your face!)

God bless you Mum.

Yours friend

TOMAS SANTOS

BUCKINGHAM PALACE

28th November, 2002

Dear Mr Santos,

The Queen wishes me to write and thank you for your letter. I am sorry to say we have no record of receiving your earlier letter, but I hope that your mother is now in good health.

It was kind of you to write to Her Majesty, but I am afraid that because of the many similar requests that are received, The Queen has had to make it a rule only to give a photograph or a signed photograph to people known personally to her.

I am returning the stamped addressed envelope that you kindly enclosed, and thank you very much for writing.

Yours sincerely,

J. Chenda Elton

Lady-in-Waiting

2 Nevill Gardens
Hove, BN3 7QF

14st January 2003

Miss R. Elton John
Lady-in-Waiting
Buckingham Palace
The Mall
(Near the roundabout)
London

Dear Miss Elton John

Thank you that you had respondered my letter on 28rd November 2002. Please forgive me to reply in a lately fashion. I had come just from my home land that I had some the 'family problems' (I think the Queen shall know what I am talking).

I observed in yours letter that the Queen should not sent any photograph only if a person should be 'known personally to her'. The best idea will be that I visit to London and pop in for the chat such that the Queen shall then know me. She can sit on her throne and give me a picture, or I can snap her with my disposable camera. Do not alarmed that I may occupy some hours – I can be extremely abrupt. I will conclude my prattle with the cup of tea in the English mood and then shall I go away.

I am busy for February although I could squeeze her in March. Thursday 27st March is suitible so I shall come to Buckingham Palace at 10.35.

Will brown shoes be OK?

Yours friend

TOMAS SANTOS
(Man-in-Waiting)

TO CELEBRATE OF CHRISTMAS

Christmas of England start always in August with glad cards in the shop, Yule logs, snowings, Santa Christmas, minces pie, hot log fires, and the Cratchits. Gay choir boys sing festival songs such that: *O Holy Nightie*, *Dig Dog Merrily on High*, and *O Little Town of Bedlam*. So put the muled wine, get a bulge in your stockings, and have the happy Christmas – for Christ's sake.

THE DISCOURSE

Yo ho ho! Merry Christmas, Darling.

Take of that stupid beard; you are six days too much soon. Have you been in the pub all morning?

Do not scold at me, Beryl. See, I have bring you some of important beer.

Oh you really are the end, Dick. Put those bottle in the refridge and come to help me embellishment the tree.

Where are the shinings, the candles, the luminances, the pretty strings, the glister balls, and the glossy trivialities?

In the box.

How shall I hang them? You have no suspenders.

You must dangle it with the filaments, such as last year.

No. I shall supervision the lightings, for I am man.

Your secret is safe with me.

No, it has true. I bring of the bacon; I am the hunter-gather; I put beard on the table; I am *Homo erectus*.

I heard rumours. Look, take the tea cosy of your head and make something to help me.

Oy vay! This tree have many pricks.

Well, it takes to know one, Sugar.

No, this have serious, Beryl. There are a bit much lot of pricking spikes. It hurted me. I shall put the gloves.

Just the minute. Those are my ovens glove. Return him at once in the kitchen room, if you don't not mind.

Right then, I shall just suffer hurtful arms to assist you.

And please turn down my sausage while you are in there.

How much degree?

Gas mask four.

Is the tree trunk progressed?

Hang on a memento, what now are you drinking?

It is little of gin and I.T.

It's a half a pint!

Beryl, this fairy have bad legs.

Never mind of the fairy's legs. You'd have bad legs, stuck there with six inches of Noble Fir up your jacksie. Get on and inspection those lights.

I shall hang up them.

Do not yet hang of it. Did you assay already thems?

Nay.

You must put him then in the power hole for test his operation.

Right. Make ready of youself; I put the electrocution in it. Three, too, one... Oh mother's love! They are defected. There is no gleam.

Yes, like every year. You need remove each blub one by at a time and put him a good one in his cavity.

Oh wait now. I have observed what it. They was not clicked of the button in the outlet. So prepare again you. Three, to, one...

Oh God of heaven! What burst in flash? Are you well, Dick? Your head is blackened and your hairs prick up.

It erupted. It discharged. My sock makes smoke and I have severe torment of the arms. But I am hale and yet alive.

Was your hands watery?

Hush now, Beryl. Can you hear of the bells and fruity Christmas songs outdoors.

It perhaps is the Salivation Army in the snow with his lamps on a stick, and brass musicians.

Brass monkeys you mean.

Hear Dick, they croon of Hark the Herald Angles Sign. That was the song of Big Crosby. It is absolutely romance of the season to see the snowy, to skate of the pond and admire to the twinkles, to taste of spicy Yule cake, and be of your goodly fellowship.

Make me then a kiss Beryl, under the mistle.

No thank you. You smell of the ashcan.

Yes. I had a sneaky cigar of the pub.

Would you like some minge pie?

Is hot?

Yes.

Give it.

Merry Xmas, Dick.
And Good Year, Babe.

Useful sayings of Christmas

Jiggle bells.
Three wise men kings.
No rooms in the in.
Baby Jesus is in the manager.
Gold, Frankincest, and myrrh.
Brandy butler.
Your crackers.
More sprouts anyone?
Will somebod please open of a widow.

A CORRESPONDENCE TO THE SALIVATION ARMY

2 Nevill Gardens
Hove, BN3 7QF

28nd Febryuary 2002

General John Gowans
The Salivation Army
101 Queer Victoria Street
London
EC4P 4EP

Dear General Gowans

Hello.

I am visit in England since a short while to learned English. Near my language
college I saw playing the band with the horn in their Salivation Army costume.
Yours dress is so excellent, General, that I wish I can wear also it and fight in the
Salivation Army with violence. Please write me at once how I can get in yours
army to learn more better to stick the knife in. Do not worry that I have the thick
glasses and my ear is broken, because I can pump ironing in the gym. I bet you
ten quids also I can drank you under a table in a twinkling. That's what my land
lord's daughter said.

He who dares winds, John, so up and smite them!

Onward Christain solders!

God bless.

Yours friend

Tomas Santos

TOMAS SANTOS

The Salvation Army

International Headquarters

101 QUEEN VICTORIA STREET
LONDON EC4P 4EP
Telephone: 0207-332 0101
Fax: 0207-236 4981
A registered charity

OFFICE OF
THE GENERAL

6 March 2002

Mr Tomas Santos
2 Nevill Gardens
Hove BN3 7QF

Dear Mr Santos,

This is to acknowledge receipt of your letter of 28 February addressed to General John Gowans, to which I am replying on the General's behalf.

I regret to say that you have been totally misled about The Salvation Army: The Salvation Army is a Christian church, and our only enemy is the Evil One, Satan; we are not a military force of any sort.

If you wish to have spiritual help, your nearest Salvation Army officer will be delighted to advise you and pray with you.

May God bless you and give you peace.

Yours sincerely,

(Laurence Hay)
Colonel
Executive Secretary to the General

WILLIAM BOOTH
Founder

JOHN GOWANS
General

OF THE FARMS YARD

On the farm jolly farmers do not soil themselves. They have hands to do it. They sit on their corn patch and rejoice to see another bringing in the sheaves at Lammastide. The farmer wife made always the cooking with fresh creams, fatty bacons, and a red face. With these, and hot sun shine, a farmer has ever the well state of health.

THE DISCOURSE

Good day, O sanguine farmer. What of your farmstead?

Mind the dung hill, friend…

Oh shucks! Right in it.

You should put the gumboot round here, old boy. How is your sandals?

Forget them. Show me your holding.

Very well. Follow me through my cow shack.

Wow! Your facility is a huge. Tell me, is that grain silo yonder belong you?

No. That is Farmer Guggins of next door. He is bad farmer. His corns are blighted of negligence and his outhouses destitute of the whitewash. He has also an unsightly blue erection for two years in his cabbage bed, which may dangerous.

Bad karma.

Come, I must now supervise the oil seed harvest and visit in my rape area.

The pasture is indeed mighty yellow.

Yes, that is the way of their efflorescence.

Excuse me, farmer, why is your dog makes a lot yap. He so excited that he licks my face and pants.

The Guggins boy always pokes his balls through a hole in the hedge and Rover wishes the game so he made snarling.

Has not his father some control of the boy? Does he not follow of the country code to made a example behaviour?

No. Indeed he has not authority fully even of his own animals and his cock is on the rampage again. He has come through the hole in my barn, and he has riddled my cider press with his pecker.

How reprehensible.

This morning he came suddenly through the farmhouse window and made my wife to jump when she was creating pie.

Farmer Guggins?

No, his cock.

You should chop of his head and made him to a soup.

Farmer Guggins?

No, his bird.

Oh.

What other bucolic items must you do today?

Well, I will tup of my rams in the south meadow, comb my silage, and inspect my mangels in the wurzel clamp. Then comes the veterinary to examine at my cow for the udder fly. He is expert; he got a medal for it.

Does he get always a pat on the back?

I suppose. After the lunch I must cut also the coat hairs of the sheep, mow the fields with a tractor, slaughter the fatling, ream my dibber, and lubricate my seed drill in the insemination unit. I must churn the butter, harvest of my plums, and broadcast the germs.

You are very much working. Will you winnow also?

He is yesterday.

I say my dear fellow, that reminded to me: can you grow me once more a fat bird for Christmas?

Will you have a grouse or shall I goose you again, Sir?

I should prefer take the turkey if is possible.

Yes, I can do it if you will assist me here now to do some things to my horse.

OK. What his name? He is so pretty I shall do it with pleasure.

Shag the pony.

Pardon?

He is so called. Here, put his harness.

Oh. Right.

Now draw him up the orchard and allow him graze. During the duration, take this auger and bore some tit holes in the bird house of the blasted oak.

Little ones?

Big ones.

Shall the pony bite on me?

No, he is soft. I have castrated his regions. If he became skittish show him this knife.

Good one.

I am now going in the near stable to inseminate the mare with

my three hands. If you are afterwards needful of a thing, you shall find me fencing in the mead.
Touché.

USEFUL SAYINGS OF THE FARM

Slurry with a fringe on top.
Do you sell firelighters?
Stable the yearling.
Beware a bull with the horn.
Are you being served?

A CORRESPONDENCE TO A BLACK ROD

2 Nevill Gardens
Hove, BN3 7QF

25 October 2002

Gentleman Usher of the Black Rod and Sergeant at Arms to the House of Lourdes
Place of Westminster
London
SW1

Dear Black Rod

I hope you shall forgive it that I had contracted you. My teacher English has told
that it is suitable to write you even that you are the important and I am the unknown
fellow.

May you to answer some my question?

- What matter is yours 'rod' constructed of?
- Is it that you must ever to wear the ornamented dress (such that you are in the
  bus?)
- Did you became some time the nervous to bang the royal knockers for
  Parlimaint?

May you to send the singed photograph in your garments? I had put the stamp for
good maners.

All the best, Black.

Yours friend

TOMAS SANTOS

GENTLEMAN USHER OF THE
HOUSE OF LORDS LONDO

TEL: O2O-7219 31
FAX: O2O-7219 2
Email: willcocksm@par

25 October 2

Dea Mr Santos,

Thank you for your letter of the 24th October 2002. I enclose a signed photograph as requested. The answer to your questions in order are:

- ❖ Ebony;
- ❖ Only when the House of Lords is actually sitting for business;
- ❖ No.

The very best of luck with your English lessons!!

Your sincerely,

Michael Willcock

GENTLEMAN USHER OF THE BLACK ROD

Tomas Santos Esq
2 Nevill Gardens
Hove
BN3 7QF

ON THE RAILROAD TRAIN

The UK train was painted of a jolly livery and can go to fast speeds everywhere. But now not. There is no more cheerful buffet car, but speed strictures, cancelling, and delaying. Of steam; of whistles; of brass buttons; of leather seat; of branches lines, and of flowers pot, all now are gone, from Dr Beeching. But welcome instead asset strippings, plastic trains, impure graffiti, burned stations, and chaos. All abroad!

THE DISCOURSE

Good day, Miss. I wish purchase the ticket to go at once in Edinburgh. How much it?

We have leafs on the railroad and insufficient drivers. Also is there de-railing at Maynard Keynes. The train therefore is cancellated.

Tsk. I will go then in Birmingham and change.

Then I must send you to Coventry.

OK, I shall transfer me. Hurry so.

No. That train is pre-occupied.

No chairs?

Twenty chairs merely.

Tsk. Well, OK, I'll have one of that. How much it?

£152.66.

That's daylight rubbery.

Look, they tickets is prime rate, Sir.

Oh glory! Have you no other?

I have a meagre few of £79. They are second rate.

Why did you not did proffer this one just now?

For Chris's sake! Are you always this rude? Your stage-coach travels away in merely little minutes and you are banding words. Do you want it or not?

Here, take it of my card.

We cannot allow Visa.

Miss, did you perhaps learned customers service by Catherine the Great?

Please not become acerbic, Sir. My credit engine has gone down on me.

But howsabout us poor passengers?

Customers.

Tsk. So, the most budget fare is £79?

Ah. You did not specific the bargain tariff. I can get you a Virgin for £30.

Just give me the billet and I will ride a Virgin for cash.

Voila. You see: there is more than one way to sink a cat.

Pshaw!

Sir, your train is now withdrawing of the station.

Oh cuss!

This window is closing.

USEFUL SAYINGS ON THE RAILROAD

Make attention Station Master: your bogies rattle.

The heatment not runs in your pullman car.
These trains once more are again behind 45 minutes.
Porter! Carry of my baggages like a good chap.
Oh, I have coal smuts on my frock coat.
Filthy washings closet!
Night Mail.

A CORRESPONDENCE TO
THE LOST PROPERTY

2 Nevill Gardens
Hove, BN3 7QF

3st December 2002

The Manger
Transports Lost Property Orifice
200 Baker Street
London NW1

Dear Sir

I had today travelled in yours Undergruond train because I had in Harrods bought a elephant's leg (for putting walking sticks).

Unfortunally, when I jumped off the train I struck a old lady with my umbrella and some plastic grapes fell of hers hat and all at once the doors closed with strong force. At this moments I instantaneously recollected my leg that I left him on the train. I looked in the widow and I could see my leg toppling everywhere and he rolled all over everybod that they were running away with fears. Then the train disappeared fast in the burrow and my leg was gone.

My leg is approximately a half a metre tall and with a skin to the coloration of grey flesh. Fortunally, I inscribed my land lord's post code on one my toenails with a ultra-violent pen. Also inside my leg is there an edition *The Lady* and one bag smoky bacon crisps. So you can not mixed him up with all the other ones you get.

Has some body put my leg in your shop? If it is, shall you sent me so I can get stuffed, or must I collect him?

I put the stamp for good responding maners.

Yours friend

[signature]

TOMAS SANTOS

Our Ref: M/12

Lost Property Office

200 Baker Street
London NW1 5RZ

Open Monday to Friday
0900 –1400
(Bank Holidays excepted)

13 December '02

Dear Sir or Madam

I am sorry to inform you that the property for which you enquired
cannot be traced.

Yours faithfully

MANAGER
LOST PROPERTY OFFICE

PERFECTLY ENGLISH PROVREBS

Many truth shall be in a provreb for the best things come with small packets. Here are a few famuos ones.

PROVREBS

If it is not busted, not repair them.

Do not examine at a gratuitous horse in hers throat.

Too much cooks damage the salad.

Do not tell the book on his wrappings.

A saved money is a gained money.

The penis bigger than the sword.

Wrestling have, wrestling edge.

It takes to understand one.

It is full with it.

It places itself.

It has what came its.

Do not think that all you read the newspapers.

It is not finished while the big lady sings.

Do not put your ovaries in a wisket.

Undo it to do it, undo it to fat.

Do not sum your hens before they came out.

Do not eat with the mouth full.

A held bird is better that two in the hedge.

Make with others because would make you make them with you.

A CORRESPONDENCE TO THE GAME SHOW

'Sesquipedalia'
2 Nevill Gardens
Hove, BN3 7QF

20sd February 2003

Richard Whiteley
Cuntdown
Channel 4 Television
124 Horseferret Road
London
SW1P 2TX

Dear Richard

Best wishes.

I am visiting in UK since a short and I was immediately interested yours TV show, *Countdwon* to improve to my language skills. My teacher English described that *Coundtown* is the first one TV show for Chanel Number 4 in UK. Moveover, you are the first man which appeared. I think you will be there *for ever*. In any case, everybody agreed that you are thoroughly 'The Biggest Cult on TV,' and I think so even if yours jacket made the test card go wobbly. My favoured game is *The Countdown Conundom* that is the anagram and I made three intersting ones:

- THE WIRY HERALDIC
- WET LID HIERARCHY
- WHY I HIT DR CEREAL

All them made: RICHARD WHITELEY.

So Richard, I have began the Society to protected the English grammar from the grammars vandal (e.g. John Prescott). Ours club is named Grammar Under Fire (GUF). Shall you wish to become ours patron? Yours title shall be Chief Guffer and you get a medallion. You must made merely one speech in a year and you can just do your usual one: 'How To Take Care Ferrets'. We can made you the salary absolutely £13 (that it is the charty work). Can you send me the singed photograph for publicity? I put the stamp for polite manners.

All the best, Richard: Diddle. Doddle. Diddly-oink – Boooiiiing!

Yours friend

TOMAS SANTOS

Very funny!

Richard Whiteley

YORKSHIRE
TELEVISION

TO COOKING

To made fine cuisine in the English kitchen you must learn to some receipts of the native chefs such that Fanny Cradock. Most favourite are: hot capons with gelatine; fishes' eggs run away in the meringue nest; peacock's skull inserted with cream; winkles on toast; and faggots on an oily bed. We have put here a facile recipe to begin you cook lessons. Observe it precisely and all your cakes will look like Fanny's.

BEEF WITH SPIT, AND LAMPREYS

1. Take a medium ox.
2. Put him to the sword.
3. Draw off his blood in a cauldron with subsequent purpose.
4. Remove of his outer vellum and destroy the fatty coat with a scratching brush. Sell this skin to a tanner for his trousers.
5. Slice away his testicles by a sharp sword. [*The ox not the tanner. Ed.*]
6. Open his interiors and dig out his heart, liver, kidney, sweetbreads, lights, bladder, chitterlings, and craw. Mummify this in your salt barrel to make afterwards a pie.
7. Peel your testicles and put them in a earthen pot. Stick them with some cloves and cover by eighteen pecks of malmsey. Boil them hard.
8. Tie your carcass with wires and put your spit in him.

Lay on honey outside and make a frottage with salts. Roast your body with a vicious flame merely an hour to shut up the vapours.

9. Take the hot meat and cut him on the kitchen's floor to extremely modest pieces. [*Takes about seven hours. Ed.*] Toss these meats into a large vessel with a spice and plums.

10. Add now of the blood and put in a brace of grouse or some rabbits.

11. Strip fifteen lampreys. Cast them also in the mush.

12. Add the testicles juice.

13. Boil yourself uncovered during eleven hours.

14. Eat it with some roots.

For a wine, choose a one with character of the young lady. She should have a well-picked nose, a robust fruity body, and a rude finish. If she is a little tart lay her in the cellar.

USEFUL SAYINGS FOR COOKINGS

A fork.
An grate cheese.
An mixture mushed up.
The sausage.
The nose of the padre.
Thighs.
Breasts.
Fruits liquidated.
Missile.

A CORRESPONDENCE TO A MUSTARD

2 Nevill Gardens
Hove, BN3 7QF

17srdnt Octember 2002

Mr Colman
Head of Mustard
Colmans of Norwich
Carrow
Norwich
NR1 2DD

Dear Mr Colman

I have eaten yours mustard to introduce my intestines to the English foods. She is the wonderful yellow liquid but my land lord had it in the tube and I thought he was a tooth paste. Oh dear. This made me dance with the fiery mouth and my hat fell off.

What made him such intensity?

Yours friend

TOMAS SANTOS

Brooke House
Manor Royal
Crawley
West Sussex
RH10 2RQ

Telephone 01293 648000

October 28, 2002   REF: CRS/ 0596305A

Mr T Santos
2 Nevill Gardens
HOVE, East Sussex
BN3 7QF

Dear Mr Santos,

Thank you for your recent letter from which we were delighted to learn how much you enjoy Colman's English Mustard.

It is always very encouraging to receive a letter such as this. We are very proud of the success that this product has achieved since it's launch and we very much hope that we will be able to maintain your enthusiasm and support for it.

Whilst we cannot quote the precise ingredients we can say that it is the Mustard Flour that we use along with the other ingredients, like spices that makes it a hot mustard.

We do appreciate the time that you have taken in writing to us. Feedback such as yours is invaluable in the continuous development of our brands and we have passed a copy of your letter onto our Marketing Department.

We hope that all future purchases will be to your complete satisfaction.

Yours sincerely

Pauline Sparkes (Mrs)
Consumer Services Advisor

2 Nevill Gardens
Hove, BN3 7QF

2rd November 2002

Pauline Sparkes Mrs
Consumper Srvices Advisor
Colmans of Crawley
Brooke House
Manor Royal
Crawley
West Sussex
RH10 2RQ

Dear Sparkes Mrs

My teeth has gone yellow.

Best wishes Sparkes Mrs.

Yours friend

TOMAS SANTOS MR

POST MORTEM BY TOMAS SANTOS

Celebrations! You are finnish. I take from my hat to you for you now are equipped of a new tongue to have intercourse with any aborigine. From my book you learned to drop your pants at the tailor and have a leek in your soup. Should you now bump on another English somebody, you have felicitous chatter on the tit of your tongue and shall not talk of cross porpoises. If you wish made the toilet in England – and are not know 'am I "gentleman?"' or 'am I "lady"?' – you now can go at once in the rightful cubicle and not fall between two stools. In your vacation, in the hostel, or in the cricket game, you have mastered the knack to introduce yourself into a man or a woman – or even a monarch.

So, at once, opportunity knocks, for all mens esteem a opportunity to made successful. But take careful: do not seem flaunt yourself such as the cocksure smarty-pants, for the Englishman will scoff a clever Dick. Furthermore, do not buy your friends another cheap languge book that is rubbish, give them this one.

Ultimately, I hope you will success, so cheerio to your good health, and up your bottoms!

Yours friend

TOMAS SANTOS